Crea

Career Portfolio

At-a-Glance Guide for Dietitians
2nd Edition

Anna Graf Williams, Ph.D.

Karen J. Hall, M.S.

Kyle Shadix, CCC, MS, RD

D. Milton Stokes, PhD, MPH, RD, CDN

LEARNOVATION

#theyoucatalyst

Learnovation, LLC
Fishers, IN 46038

Editor in Chief: Anna Graf Williams, Ph.D.
Production and Development Editor: Karen J. Hall
Copy Editor: Cheryl Pontius

Printed in the United States of America

10 9 8 7 6 5 4 3 2 1

ISBN 978-0-9969528-0-4

LEARNOVATION
#theyoucatalyst

Learnovation®, LLC
Fishers, IN 46038

www.learnovation.com

Contents

Step 3: Create Your Résumé and Your Online Presence 69

Step 4: Assembling Your Career Portfolio 97

PREFACE

It's a great time to be in the dietetic field!

In 2012, the government reported the employment of 67,400 dietitians and nutritionists across the country. By 2022, this figure is expected to climb to 81,600. The field of dietetics is expected to grow over 20% in the next five years as a result of an increased emphasis on wellness, public interest in following a healthier lifestyle, and advances in science and medicine. Retiring baby boomers are seeing the value of eating right to live longer and more active lives in retirement, and experienced dietitians and nutritionists are in demand. Dietitians are present not just in health care systems and hospitals, but are promoting healthy lifestyles in the food industry, sports medicine, research, food safety, journalism, corporate wellness, and personal coaching and consulting.

As a dietitian, you are an agent of change... and that takes not only a person skilled in the nutritional care process, but someone who has a science and food background, who can stay abreast of new trends and research and apply it to solve problems. It takes a person who can communicate in a way that makes people stop and listen, who can manage the resources and people around him or her, especially those people who really don't understand all the things a dietetic professional can do.

The field of dietetics is also supported by the Academy of Nutrition and Dietetics, and their credentialing agency, The Commission on Dietetic Registration (CDR), which sets the standards required to be a practicing dietitian. Your career path includes an exacting educational program, a competitive internship experience, a comprehensive exam, and lifelong continuing education once you have become a registered dietitian.

You've got great career potential, and one of the most important things you can do to advance your dietetic career is to begin to identify your key skills, document what you can do, promote yourself to others, and share your passion. That's where the career portfolio comes in... as a tool for capturing and sharing who you are and what you can do.

Career Portfolios Today

You've got the skills and you've got the passion for a career in dietetics. It's up to you to promote yourself and take charge of your career, whether you are gearing up to compete for a dietetic internship, starting a new rotation on your supervised practice program, getting that first job, or working on your recertification plan.

Career portfolios are an easy way to begin to collect and organize samples of your work, your community service, your projects, awards, hobbies, and materials from school to prove you have the knowledge, skills, and abilities to do the job.

Schools and universities have discovered the benefits of student portfolios as a way to prove students are learning what they need to know to earn the degree. Today, many organizations introduce students to the ePortfolio early in their school career and encourage them to continue to add samples and projects throughout their program. The new challenge facing students is not trying to find enough samples, but figuring out which ones are worth showing. Taking your career portfolio from a collection of documents to a showcase of your skills and abilities is the focus of this second edition. You'll learn how to create and use a career portfolio to advance your career.

Employers Are Looking for Talent

Today's employers no longer have to compete as hard to attract the graduates, and they have a large pool of applicants from which to choose. Hiring has changed with the integration of new technologies, the Internet, and social media. Résumés are scanned electronically for keywords, and those that make the cut may be reviewed in less than 10 seconds. Companies are looking beyond the basic requirements of the degree and looking for the specific skills that make a great employee. Human Resource departments (HR) are undergoing a shift and looking at employees not only to fill the specific dietetic position, but to provide the talent and skills required to meet company goals and projects across the organization. HR is developing a pool of talent, and they are looking for people who can meet the needs. Knowing your skills and rare talents and meeting the needs of the employer are the keys to getting the position in today's job market.

We Focus on the How-To's

In the 2nd edition of *Creating Your Career Portfolio: At-A-Glance Guide for Dietitians*, we're staying true to what we do best, focusing on giving you the how-to's of Career Portfolios to showcase your skills and talents for today's employer and internship coordinator.

- How do you identify your skills and plan for the skills you need while you're still in school?
- Where do you find work samples, and which ones do you use in different situations?
- What's the best way to show your skills and experiences gained outside of work and school?
- When do you use a hard copy portfolio and when do you use your ePortfolio?

- How can you make the most of your internship, and how can you use your career portfolio with social media to network and connect to get a job after graduating?
- How can you use your career portfolio to document your continuing learning and experiences for your PDP (Professional Development Portfolio)?

Moving Forward

We'll start this book with an introduction to the career portfolio process and then focus on five steps to creating and using Career Portfolios:

1. Identifying your skills and creating a career plan.
2. Creating and managing work samples.
3. Creating a power résumé, cover letters, and creating a good online presence.
4. Assembling your career portfolio – both hard copy and ePortfolio, for use in different situations, and creating and collecting the support materials for your career portfolio.
5. Using your career portfolio – whether you are looking for a job, competing for a dietetic internship or scholarship, or going after promotion or a raise. We look at using your hard copy portfolio to interview, and your ePortfolio to promote and network your skills.

Creating Your Career Portfolio: At-A-Glance Guide for Dietitians is a guide to moving your career ahead. **This book can help you find a focus, make a plan, and develop tools to help you succeed on the job and in the workplace.**

Downloadable Templates

A series of Microsoft Word templates are available to help you create documents for your career portfolio.

Download the template files at:
http://www.learnovation.com/d2-templates/
or scan the QR code at the right with your phone to go directly to the web site.

Use these documents as a starting point. Customize these files and make them work for you. Feel free to change the fonts and rearrange information as needed.

When a template is available you will see this icon:

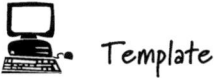

Template

The Reference section has a complete list of templates and details on downloading the file.

About the Authors

Anna Graf Williams, Ph.D.

Anna Graf Williams, Ph.D., co-founder and president of Learnovation, LLC, is a national expert on career portfolios. She has spent over 20 years standardizing the career portfolio process. The *Creating Your Career Portfolio* series has expanded to include career portfolio oriented materials including videos and targeted workbooks for students, professionals, and dietitians. She regularly speaks on the topics of career portfolios, outcomes assessment, and the holistic

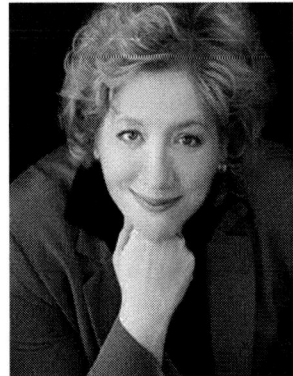

approach to job readiness. Dr. Williams has a Ph.D. in educational administration from Purdue University, along with master degrees in curriculum development and design and Restaurant Hotel Institutional Management. Dr. Williams was formerly a full professor at the collegiate level, where she specialized in Hospitality, Strategic Planning, Marketing and Curriculum Development. She has specialized throughout her educational career on innovative and effective teaching methods, outcome assessment, marketing, and management.

Dr. Williams has co-authored over 33 books including:

- *The Medical Advocate Book*
- *Creating Your Career Portfolio At-a-Glance Guide for Students 4th Ed.*
- Creating Your Career Portfolio At-a-Glance Guide BASICS.
- *Creating Your Career Portfolio At-a-Glance Guide for Professionals.*
- *Creating Your Career Portfolio At-a-Glance Guide for Dietitians.*
- *Workforce / Reentry, Financial Literacy, Wellness & Nutrition, Parenting, and Study Skills Pamphlet Series.*
- *Immigrant's Guide to the American Workplace.*
- *Family Guide to the American Workplace.*
- *Quick Reference Guide to Food Safety and Sanitation.*
- *Food Safety Fundamentals.*

Dr. Williams is also an experienced medical advocate, and teaches people how to successfully assist their loved ones by navigating and working with the many players in the health arena- including dietitians, ER doctors, insurance companies, hospitalists, hospital advocates, scheduling teams, and office nurses to name a few.

Karen J. Hall, M.S.

Karen Hall is the "how-to" specialist of the Learnovation®, LLC team. As co-founder and artistic director, Ms. Hall's focus is instructional design and product development. Over the past 20 years, she has spent time refining the mechanics of the career portfolio including the three-hour emergency instructions, templates, and ePortfolio concepts.

Ms. Hall has a master's degree in Instructional Computing from Purdue University where she specialized in instructional design and computer-assisted instruction, and a bachelor's degree in office administration from Illinois State University.

Ms. Hall has a background in corporate training, from the design and development of materials and documentation to classroom and on-site delivery. She worked as a corporate trainer for a software development company for seven years where she designed and created training programs, materials, and documentation for several different products for the nonprofit industry.

Ms. Hall is the co-author of:

- *Creating Your Career Portfolio At-a-Glance Guide for Students 4th Ed.*
- *Creating Your Career Portfolio At-a-Glance Guide BASICS.*
- *Creating Your Career Portfolio At-a-Glance Guide for Professionals.*
- *Creating Your Career Portfolio At-a-Glance Guide for Dietitians.*
- *Career Transitions Workbook.*
- *College Prep Portfolio Workbook.*
- *Workforce / Reentry, Financial Literacy, Wellness & Nutrition, Parenting and Study Skills Pamphlet Series.*
- *Family Guide to the American Workplace.*

Kyle Shadix, CCC, MS, RD

Chef Kyle Shadix is the only Certified Research Chef (CRC) in the world who is also a Registered Dietitian (MS, RD) and a Fellow of the Academy of Nutrition and Dietetics (FAND). A culinary-nutrition food scientist, Chef Kyle supports product development for PepsiCo Global R&D where he serves as the company's first Corporate Executive Research Chef for Global Beverage.

Chef Kyle was also the founder of his own agency, Nutrition & Culinary Consultants, acquired in 2006 by the WPP, the world's largest communications company. Prior to that, Kyle's food and nutrition career has spanned from the drive-in window at McDonald's in rural GA, to NYC's acclaimed Bouley & Gotham Bar & Grill. Kyle has also worked as an instructor at Columbia University, operations manager at Lehman Brothers, and at Memorial Sloan Kettering Cancer Center.

In the past, Kyle has also served as the media spokesperson for companies including Dannon, The Mayo Clinic, Netflix, Celestial Seasonings, and The United States Tea Council.

Kyle has served on the Board of the American Institute of Wine and Food, and held numerous leadership positions with the Academy of Nutrition & Dietetics and the International Association of Culinary Professionals. Kyle has received various awards and recognition such as The American Dietetic Association's NYC Recognized Young Dietitian Award, The Emily Quinn Professional Achievement Award from the University of Georgia Alumni Association and the Publix Visiting Practitioner at the University of Georgia's Department of Food and Nutrition.

Kyle is currently studying part-time for his PhD in Food Science at Rutgers University in NJ; he expects to complete the program in 2020. He received his Masters of Science in foods and nutrition from New York University, Bachelors of Science in consumer foods and foods science from the University of Georgia, Athens, and culinary training at the Culinary Institute of American, Hyde Park, & Le Cordon Bleu, Paris.

D. Milton Stokes, PhD, MPH, RD, CDN

D. Milton Stokes, PhD, MPH, RD, CDN, is a Registered Dietitian / Nutritionist, Director of Global Health & Nutrition Outreach for Monsanto Company, and owner of One Source Nutrition, LLC. He has over 20 years experience in the areas of food and nutrition as a nutrition counselor and former restaurateur.

Specializing in weight management and eating disorders, Milton's firm helps individuals and groups overcome barriers to success by offering personalized nutrition assessment and planning. Clients set actionable, attainable goals, and they learn how to transcend the lure of fad dieting and unhealthy weight loss.

In addition, Milton is a former National Media Spokesperson for the Academy of Nutrition and Dietetics where he's been featured in *Cooking Light, Fitness, Self, Men's Health, AOL, The Washington Post, Ladies Home Journal,* and countless others. He's also written freelance articles for *Environmental Nutrition, Today's Dietitian, Family Doctor, Men's Health, WeightWatchers.com, NY Daily News,* and others. His book, *Flat Belly Diet! for Men* (Rodale, 2009) is a New York Times bestseller and he is a coauthor of *Launching Your Dietetics Career.*

Milton began his career in clinical nutrition at Interfaith Medical Center in Brooklyn, NY. He has also worked at Jamaica Hospital Medical Center & Trump Nursing Home in Jamaica, Queens; North General Hospital in New York, NY; and St. Barnabas Hospital & Nursing Home in the Bronx. He has served in staff and management positions along the way as well as precepted dietetic interns and students from several area colleges and programs. His PhD is in Communication and Marketing from the University of Connecticut where he specialized in Health Communication. He holds a Masters in Public Health concentrating in Health Education from Hunter College, and his clinical training was conducted at Yale-New Haven Hospital, affiliated with Yale University School of Medicine. He can be contacted at miltonstokes@gmail.com.

CAREER PORTFOLIO BASICS

It's all about the Passion... Ask any registered dietitian why he or she chose the profession, and you will hear a different story. They might have encountered friends and family with health issues, been fascinated by the science of food, or felt the impact of nutrition on their performance as an athlete. Dietitians have a passion for what they do. Being able to showcase your skills and qualifications with that passion is the edge you need to compete for a dietetic internship or the find the right job.

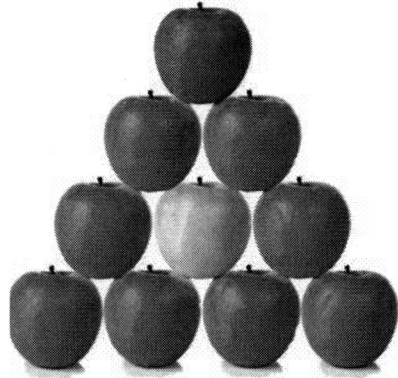

Knowing your skills and abilities, documenting your work experiences, education and community service are critical to completing your education, getting a dietetic internship and becoming a professional. A Career Portfolio is the tool you will use to identify your strengths, document your skills, and market yourself as the right person for the job.

"How do I use all my experiences to build my dietetic career?"

This book is going to tell you how to take a collection of your work and turn it into a power tool to show an internship coordinator or employer all the skills and knowledge you've developed during your career. You'll take all your projects, activities, work experiences, volunteer experiences, etc., and combine it into a tool you can use to show anyone what you can do- why you qualify for the position, the internship, the scholarship, or why you deserve the raise and what qualifies you for the promotion.

What is a Career Portfolio?

A **career portfolio** is an organized presentation of your skills, abilities, experiences, job history, and education. It is an in-depth career summary designed to showcase the best you have to offer.

You can create two different formats of a career portfolio, a **hard copy career portfolio** and an electronic version we call an **ePortfolio**. Each has its benefits and uses, and we recommend you create both types.

A career portfolio is a tool you use when you want to show someone you are the right person for...

- the job.
- the scholarship.
- the internship.
- the promotion.
- the raise.

You will collect **work samples** (sometimes called artifacts) that show all the things you can do: Your skills and abilities from all areas of your life, including your job, your education, hobbies, activities, interests, and volunteering. These samples can be documents you've created on the job, letters of recommendation, samples of projects and presentations you've done in school, videos you've created for YouTube™, educational articles you've written for a magazine, menu plans for athletic training, awards, certificates, pictures, etc.

From this collection of samples, you will decide which of your skills and abilities you want to promote about yourself, and you'll organize and assemble your career portfolio to highlight these skills. As you develop your portfolio you actual build a personal profile of your skills and qualifications.

It's a Process

Putting together your career portfolio is a process... because it's not just about the collection of documents, but what you do with them, how you organize and classify them to show someone your very best. By going through this process you get an understanding of who you are, what skills you bring to the table, your strengths and weaknesses.

You'll be taking a look at all the things you do on the job, or in your classes and then start to look at everything from a skill perspective. Instead of just doing a project because it's assigned, you'll look at the course syllabus on the first day and say "Exactly what am I getting out of this class?" How is it going to move me toward being a dietitian? What professional areas of competency am I gaining in this class? What additional skills am I developing as I work in groups, give presentations, and write this report? You'll also start seeing all the other skills you are building on the job, in your fraternity or sorority, when you do counseling, or volunteer at the 5K race.

A career portfolio is not just about including your best samples, but **it's about developing a career focus,** identifying your skills and abilities, your strengths and weaknesses, and setting goals to build your career in the dietetic field.

When you put together your career portfolio, you learn to recognize your strengths and find ways to emphasize these through your career portfolio. You are also faced with your weaknesses, and in the process, you find ways to compensate.

Learn about yourself. Some people have created a career portfolio, and then never actually showed it in an interview. But, what they learned about themselves and their capabilities helped them to talk with confidence about what they could do and what they had to offer.

It's Proof

Career portfolios are designed to help you show someone what you can do, by providing proof through the work samples you choose to share. The samples you show to a person will change depending on how you are using your career portfolio. Think of the career portfolio as your documentation... your personal marketing kit. If you have a 50% chance of getting into a dietetic internship program, what can you show that coordinator to prove you are a good match to his or her program?

It's Your Edge

Using a career portfolio can help you:

- stand out from the crowd
- show actual proof of your abilities
- get more confidence to talk about yourself in any interview situation
- get a higher starting salary by showing an interviewer why you're worth more
- show your organization skills
- market yourself

- help interviewers see your specialized skills and interests and how you can fit into the organization.

Ace the interviews– Most people dread internship and job interviews. The spotlight is on you and you don't always know what the interviewer is looking for with their questions and comments. **Once you've put together your career portfolio, you'll know with confidence the answers to the tough interview questions.** You will know your skills inside and out and be able to show examples of what you can do for the employer and why you are the right person for the job.

Career Portfolios in Hard Copy Format

A **hard copy career portfolio** is a 3-ring binder that contains all your documents and samples in an organized way. All your work samples and documents are put in sheet protectors and organized by tabs to focus on the key skills you want to promote.

Here are a few things you should know about the hard copy format:

- **It is used in a personal interview** to show actual samples of your work and copies of your certificates, awards, etc.
- **It is NOT a scrapbook** of everything you've done, it's a collection of your best work.
- **It's easy to customize for an interview–** just swap different samples in and out of the binder.
- **You don't have to have computer access** during the interview.
- **A hard copy career portfolio has a great pass around factor.** If you have several people in the interview, your career portfolio may take a tour of the room– giving your samples some good exposure and creating talking points for you.

Career Portfolios in Electronic Format

An **ePortfolio** is an electronic version of your career portfolio that can be viewed on a computer, a phone, or tablet. There are many different ePortfolio programs you can use, and they all have different features and functions.

Many schools today provide students with the software and computer access to create an ePortfolio. The important thing to know about the program you use is how you can organize your samples and information and then customize what can be shared with someone else who would be viewing your ePortfolio.

Sometimes your ePortfolio can become a junk drawer, with all kinds of things thrown into it. Making sure your drawer is organized makes it easier to quickly find what you need.

It also helps to be able to take a few specific things out of the drawer to show to someone else. A person reviewing your academic records for an internship may not need to see your life guard certificate, but an employer for a summer job might. Being able to select what someone sees is critical when using your ePortfolio effectively.

Benefits of Having an ePortfolio

- You can store all your work samples electronically– it's a good way to keep track of all your samples
- You have flexibility in how you group your work samples together. It's easy to show one work sample and have it linked to different skills.
- You can e-mail someone a hyperlink so they can view only the information you choose.
- ePortfolios are often used before an interview as a way to generate interest in you, or after the interview to remind people of what you have to offer.

- More initial interviews are being conducted over the phone or in video conference chats and webinars. Being able to show parts of your ePortfolio or being able to send a file via e-mail can give the interviewer quick access to key information.
- ePortfolios are sometimes used in interview settings, to show select samples on a tablet.

Electronic and hard copy career portfolios complement each other. Together they can keep your career on track. Many schools use ePortfolios as a way to track and document the success of their programs and class outcomes, but may not be as easy to customize for display. If you already have an ePortfolio from school, you'll learn some good ways to select, organize, and present your samples. Knowing what to do with the information being tracked is part of designing a good Career ePortfolio. We'll be looking at the best ways to create and use both electronic and hard copy career portfolios throughout the book.

You need a hard copy career portfolio and an ePortfolio to showcase your skills

The Contents of a Career Portfolio

A career portfolio is designed to show people proof that you have the skills and abilities you want to promote.

When you create a hard copy portfolio, you will be assembling your documents and work samples into a 3-ring binder, with tabs separating the key sections of your career portfolio.

When you create an electronic portfolio, you want to select what portions of your ePortfolio a person can view, and what specific work samples to show. The amount of control you have over how your ePortfolio displays content varies greatly between programs. You may have to be creative about how you label and set up documents in order to include some items in your career portfolio.

Here's a list of the key parts of a career portfolio in the order they appear in a hard copy portfolio:

Items with this icon ⌷ are **tabbed sections** of the career portfolio.

Items with this icon ▤ are **pages** in the career portfolio.

Basic Contents of a Career Portfolio

▤ **Statement of Originality & Confidentiality**
(one page that lets people know this is your work and asks them not to copy it.)

▷ **TAB 1: Work Philosophy & Goals.**

   ▤ **Work Philosophy** (Your beliefs about yourself, people, and your outlook on work. Use three to five bullet points.)

   ▤ **Goals** (Your career goals for the next two to five years. Use three to five bullet points.)

   ▤ **Professional Bio** (A brief overview of who you are.)

▷ **TAB 2:** ▤ **Résumé.**

▷ **TAB 3: Key Skill Area 1:**

   ▤ 3-5 Work samples for your most important skill.

▷ **TAB 4: Key Skill Area 2:**

   ▤ 3-5 Work samples for another skill area.

▷ **TAB 5: Key Skill Area 3:**

   ▤ 3-5 Work samples for another skill area.

▷ **TAB 6: Additional Resources** - includes the following items:

   ▤ **Faculty & Employer Bio Sheet** (Brief descriptions of the people whose names appear in your career portfolio - who they are and what they do.)

   ▤ **Academic Plan of Study** (A copy of your plan of study listing the courses you have taken to fulfill your degree, if applicable.)

   ▤ **References** (A list of people who can verify your character, academic record, or employment history.)

You Can ADD MORE

This is the basic list. Now, KEEP IN MIND... Depending on *your* work samples, experience, involvement, and education, you may choose to have MORE tabs than this basic list.

You might want to add additional tabs such as:

- 📂 **Volunteerism / Community Service** (Work samples, letters of recognition, photos of projects completed, programs and brochures relating to community service projects, and/or volunteer experience.)

- 📂 **Certifications, Diplomas, Degrees, Scholarships, and Awards** (Copies of documents.)

- 📂 **Memberships** (Membership cards, citations, photos, and letters related to organizations.)

- 📂 **Works in Progress** (Examples of projects and materials that may not be complete, but you want to show off.)

You Can HAVE LESS

If you don't have enough samples to fill up a tabbed section, you might have fewer Key Skill Areas, or need to combine two Key Skill Areas into one. You might need to include some of your certificates or community service samples in one of your Key Skill Areas instead of keeping it under a separate tab. Remember, it's *your* career portfolio, designed to show your best work, so we'll be looking at the best ways to showcase everything you have to offer.

We'll be going into much more details on the contents of a career portfolio when we look at the details of work samples and assembling a career portfolio.

Make it Real.

Your career portfolio should reflect who you are right now. Don't pad it with filler projects and samples if you don't have them. Take a look at what you're missing, and make plans to fill the gaps.

The Five Steps to Developing a Career Portfolio

There are five steps to developing your career portfolio:

1. **Knowing your skills and planning your career–** Identifying your current skills, your target career and jobs, and the gap between the two. Plan for gaining the skills and knowledge you need to move forward by setting goals.

2. **Collecting and organizing your work samples–** Work samples are the guts of your career portfolio. The actual proof you use to show you have the skills to do the job. Your samples are what set you apart from other people; they show what you have to offer. Work samples are the proof of all the things you can do, from all parts of your life. We'll look at the types of samples you can use, where to find them, and how to capture and keep track of all these samples. We'll look at how to categorize and organize your work samples to show the best of what you do.

3. **Creating Your Résumé–** We often say that **your résumé gets you the interview, your career portfolio gets you the job.** If your career portfolio is your marketing kit, your **résumé** is the one-page summary to who you are and what you have to offer. You'll learn

how to create a résumé that really focuses on your skills and highlights your qualifications, and makes employers want to interview you for the internship or position. Then we'll look at ways to use social media and LinkedIn™ to promote your skills and network with people who can help advance your career.

4. **Assembling the Career Portfolio**- We'll look at how to customize a career portfolio to showcase your skills in a job interview, promotion, or compete for internships and scholarships. You'll learn how to combine your work samples and other key documents into an electronic and a hard copy career portfolio, making sure your career portfolio is customized to each person reviewing your work.

5. **Using the Career Portfolio**- We'll look at ways to use your hard copy career portfolio and your ePortfolio in interviews and as a marketing tool. You'll learn how to customize your electronic and hard copy career portfolio for different settings, from job interviews and reviews, to applying for colleges or internships, tracking certifications, or competing for scholarships. You'll be creating the tool for keeping a pulse on your career now and in the future.

So, let's jump in and get started with Step 1: Knowing Your Skills and Planning Your Career.

Step 1:
Know Your Skills
& Plan Your Career

Getting A Career Focus

In Step 1 we're going to take a hard look at the actual knowledge, skills, and abilities (called KSA's) you have now, and what you're learning in school or on the job. What kind of job can you get right now? What experiences have you had that can help you as a dietitian? You'd be surprised to know how many skills you do have because we're not just talking about the jobs you've had or the classes you've taken. You're going to really inventory your skills: from volunteer service, activities, hobbies, and interests, to the leadership, time management, negotiation or speaking skills you don't always learn on the job or in the classroom. Next, you'll look at the field of dietetics, identify your ideal job, and compare your current skills to your target position, and identify the gaps. You'll look at what you need, and then make a plan for reaching your goals.

Why Do We Care So Much About Skills?

Your skills and abilities are your ticket to getting a dietetic internship and a job. Employers are looking for people who have the skills needed to do the job, but they expect you to bring a lot more skills than just the technical skills of being a dietitian You're expected to be able to solve problems, to organize your time, to be able to teach someone else a process,

> **Your skills and abilities are your ticket to getting a job.**

communicate with others inside and outside the company, and work as a team. You're expected to bring a good work ethic, and an attitude that says you want to be there and you want to do this job.

The reality is that with a shortage of dietetic internship opportunities each year, almost half of the graduates of a didactic program won't be able to find a supervised practice program and will have to find other alternatives to practice in their field. There are plenty of people looking for that same opportunity. What makes you the right person for the program? What do you bring to the company that the other people don't have?

To get the job you really want, you have to have the right skills, training or education, and the experience required for the job. Your career portfolio is a tool you will use showcase your experiences and market yourself.

It's all about having the right skills to do the job.

There are three parts to Step 1... taking stock of your current skills, identifying your career path, and then identify the gaps and make the plan for reaching your career goals.

1. **Identify Your Skills–** Exactly what can you do right now? What skills would you promote to an employer, and how would you prove you have those skills? We'll take inventory and classify your current skills and experience.

> **Step 1:**
> 1. Identify Your Skills.
> 2. Identify Your Target Career and Jobs.
> 3. Create Your Career Plan.

2. **Identify Your Target Career and Jobs–** What's your ideal job look like? With so many areas where you can practice as a dietitian, what job do you see yourself doing when you graduate? What

additional training will you need to obtain a specialty certification? You'll take a look at the knowledge, skills and abilities needed to do the job.

3. **Create Your Career Plan**– Look at your target career and compare it to your current skills. Where is the gap? What's missing? More education? More experience? A certification in a specialty? You'll figure out what you need, create your route for getting that target job, and set your career goals. Now, on to the first part...

Part 1- Identify Your Skills

"Why Should I Hire You?"

"What makes you the right person for the job?"

These don't have to be hard questions in an interview. It's time to stop and take a personal inventory of all your skills and what you can do right now.

So, just what are employers looking for?

- People who have the knowledge and skills to do the job.
- People who have the ability to learn.
- People whose interests, values, and work style fit with the company.

The power of your career portfolio is the ability to show examples and proof of your various skills, knowledge, and abilities that will make you a good candidate. Let's start with a few terms you need to know:

- **KNOWLEDGE**– something you have learned or discovered.
- **SKILL**– the ability to perform a task- usually something learned.
- **ABILITY**– qualities that enable you to perform a task - something you have within you that helps you do the skill.

- **COMPETENCY**– the capability to apply or use a set of related knowledge, skills, and abilities required to successfully perform "critical work functions" or tasks, in a defined work setting.

Knowledge comes from education, training, or experience. You can take a class, you watch someone do something, you read about it.

Skill is the ability to perform a task - whether that is riding a bike, creating a menu, surfing the Internet, performing surgery, making a speech, or managing a team.

Ability is something you have that helps you perform the task. The physical strength to lift boxes, being able to read and write, being able to pay attention, or being able to do math to give back change.

Competency is being able to do productive work using your knowledge, skills, and abilities. A job description is a group of competencies you need to do a specific job. Employers look at you to see what knowledge, skills, and abilities you can bring to a job. Do you have the physical ability to do the job? Do you have the background knowledge and skills to do the job well? Do you have the ability to learn new things and problem solve in this job? Knowledge, skills and abilities are often abbreviated as **KSAs.**

Know your KSAs - (Knowledge, Skills & Abilities)

ACEND® Standards

A high set of competencies have been developed for professionals in dietetics. If you are in school right now working towards a degree as a registered dietitian or a dietetic technician, you should be in a program that has been certified by the Accreditation Council for Education in Nutrition and Dietetics (ACEND®.) ACEND® requires that students who graduate meet the requirements in the following five knowledge areas called **KRDs**:

KRD 1: Scientific and Evidence Base of Practice – You can do research into dietetic topics and put the research into practice through projects, experiments, reports, and analysis.

KRD 2: Professional Practice Expectations – You know how to communicate with people, both in writing and verbally, in ways that help people create positive change. You follow ethical guidelines and act like a professional.

KRD 3: Clinical and Customer Services – You know the nutritional care process and can use it effectively to make decisions, identify problems, diagnose solutions, implement, evaluate, and monitor situations. These are the core skills that distinguish a dietitian from other professionals.

KRD 4: Practice Management and Use of Resources –It takes more than just understanding nutrition to be a dietitian. You need to be able to manage financial resources, and people; understand food service operations and food safety; follow public policy and regulations related to dietetics; follow regulations related to health care; and use the coding and billing of dietetics/nutrition services.

KRD 5: Support Knowledge –You must have the core courses in foods science, organic chemistry, biology, psychology, sociology, etc. that serve as the foundation for dietetics.

Each area includes a list of competencies (CRD) that give the specific requirements you should be able to do as a dietitian. Being able to classify your knowledge and skills into these five standard areas is critical. Each work sample you include in your career portfolio should show how you meet and exceed these standards. **We will be using the ACEND® standards as a way of categorizing work samples to document your abilities in the dietetic field.** A listing of the ACEND® standards for certified dietitians can be found in the Resources section on page 183.

ACEND® standards are in place to protect you as a professional and tell others that you have the qualifications to do the job. Professionals in the field have helped to set these standards of performance, and they continue to be updated each year. Every class you take in your dietetic program has to identify which standards are being met in that class. You will also need to demonstrate your competency in each area as part of your dietetic internship.

> ### ACEND® Knowledge Areas, Competencies and Work Samples
>
> Here is an example of one knowledge area, a corresponding competency, and possible work sample that demonstrates the skill:
>
> **KRD 2** The curriculum must include opportunities to develop a variety of communication skills sufficient for entry into pre-professional practice.
>
> **CRD 2.3** Design, implement, and evaluate presentations to a target audience.
>
> **Work sample:** A video of a presentation given on healthy weight loss options.

Types of Skills

All your past experiences have been preparing you to enter the workplace. Even classes that you didn't like, or the ones you thought were boring gave you information and skills you can use on the job. Those skills come in the form of:

Technical skills– specific tasks you can perform to do a job, like the ability to plan a menu for people with diabetes, correctly coding a patient billing statement for an insurance claim, or working with food allergies. **Soft skills**– your people skills, such as communicating and negotiating, managing your time or multi-tasking. Motivating people to make a change in their diet, avoiding conflict, or providing comfort to a patient in a difficult situation are all marketable skills that can help you on a job or as you go for more advanced training and education.

You are also constantly building your **transferable skills**– the skills that can help you in different jobs and situations. The public speaking skills you learned in your speech class can help you give a presentation to your boss on the job, or help you promote healthy snacks to students during final exam week. Being able to show patience at your own doctor's appointment, can help you be patient with a difficult client. Transferable skills can be hard or soft skills.

Technical Skills

Technical skills or "hard skills" are physical things you can do or special knowledge you have to do a task or solve a problem. You are learning new technical skills all the time, whether you're taking a class, working on the job, or hanging out with friends. Here are some examples of technical skills in dietetics:

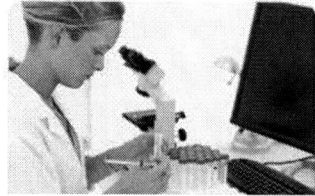

Sample Technical Skills

Food preparation
- Menu formulation
- Food preparation
- Purchasing.

Food safety
- Knowledge of health, safety, and issues related to food consumption trends
- Nutrient composition of foods, food additives, food allergies and hypersensitivities
- Naturally occurring toxins, pathogens, pesticides, biotechnology-derived foods
- Irradiated foods
- Food laws and regulations.

Assessment
- Assessment and screening techniques
- Medical record reviews
- Care plan development
- Documentation techniques.

Nutrition in disease
- Physiological and biochemical aspects of nutrition metabolism
- Biochemical and physiological principles of nutrition for sport, obesity, eating disorders, respiration, alcohol metabolism, inborn errors, immunity, cancer
- The nervous system and trauma.

As you gain technical skills, you also learn to use **tools** and **technology** to do the job.

- **TOOLS**– Machines, equipment, and tools you may use on the job.

- **TECHNOLOGY**– software and information technology used to perform a task or do a job.

Here are just a few of the tools and technologies used by a dietitian:

Tools	Technology
■ Glucometers	■ Nutritionist Pro™ software
■ Impedance meters	■ FoodWorks™ software
■ Notebook computers	■ CyberSoft NutriBase™
■ Skinfold calipers	■ Medical software
■ Calorimeters	■ Microsoft Office™

Start thinking about all the tools and technology you use every day, whether it's a spreadsheet or word processing program, editing a YouTube™ video, or posting to a blog.

Soft Skills

Soft Skills are character traits that show how well you interact with other people. They are also known as **people skills.**

Soft skills are often harder to iden-tify than technical skills, and judg-ing how well someone can do the skill varies based on the person measuring performance. Think about it... how do you measure courtesy? Different people have dif-ferent expectations. We pick up many soft skills as we grow up, and are influenced by the people around us. Soft skills are often the hardest skills to learn or improve.

A dietitian has to have a good balance of technical and soft skills. Getting the message across in a way that help people make changes is a vital skill for dietitians. Employers value individuals with excellent soft skills, because just having the knowledge and technical skill to do the job isn't enough. You have to be able to function well with others, communicate effectively, work on a team, plan, organize, manage your time, and the list goes on.

.

Sample Soft Skills

Teamwork

Being a good team member means:

- Putting the good of the team ahead of yourself
- Respecting others' opinions
- Hearing people out
- Involving everyone in finding solutions to problems.

Presentation skills

- Leading a meeting
- Promoting an idea to your boss
- Giving a presentation on healthy breakfast choices to a student group.

Communication skills

- Answering the phone
- Writing e-mails
- Writing an article for a magazine
- Interacting with co-workers and clients.

Leadership

- Heading up a project
- Training others
- Delegating
- Negotiating a contract
- Managing conflict
- Planning
- Setting priorities
- Organizing skills.

Other Soft Skills

- Problem solving
- Multi-tasking
- Thinking quickly
- Ability to make decisions
- Customer service
- Courtesy
- Ability to work with people from different cultures
- Self-discipline
- Work ethic.

The Top Six Soft Skills

- **Communication**– how we give and take in information, how we listen and speak with others.

- **Enthusiasm and attitude**– having a positive attitude in the workplace, how that impacts others, and feeling a sense of pride in your work.

- **Teamwork**– the importance of working together with others to a common goal, being an effective team member and interacting well with others.

- **Networking**– being able to talk to others, building successful business relationships with other people.

- **Problem solving and critical thinking**– how to solve problems in the workplace in a variety of ways, making ethical decisions, working with others to resolve conflicts.

- **Professionalism**– blending and integrating the other five skills.

Based on U.S. Department of Labor and industry leaders

Transferable Skills

Transferable skills are skills that you can take from one area or job and use in another. An executive in business could bring her management skills to a new career in the dietetic field. She might use many of the same skills, just in a different setting.You can take the skill of being good with people and use it in health care, social services, retail, or

other jobs. Or your knowledge as a runner may give you insight into how it feels to have a special marathon training diet. More people are finding their way to a second career in dietetics, bringing their existing skills and education from many other fields. **Transferable skills can come from:**

- different jobs
- activities you do on your own personal time
- volunteering and community service
- hobbies
- memberships
- jobs that you hold that don't seem to relate to your career.

Sometimes the common skills you have in one job may be a **rare talent,** a valuable skill that sets you apart, in another.

Transferable skills can be hard or soft skills and you don't have to get them on the job or from your education. Athletes often have transferable skills that can help them in a variety of jobs and situations:

Transferable Skills for a Soccer Player

- Determination
- Communication skills
- Performing under pressure
- Goal setting
- Dedication
- Training regimes

- Discipline
- Commitment to excellence
- Teamwork

While the technical skill of being able to kick a ball or making a great corner kick may not be in demand in the workplace (unless you are going pro,) there are many soft skills that would be valuable to a potential employer. How many of the skills listed above would help the player communicate with patients, coordinate a healthy eating campaign, or be a great sports nutrition coach?

You have a lot more skills than you think. You didn't just get skills from your classes or from a part-time job, but from participating in after-school clubs and activities, playing sports and being on a team, volunteering at a local church or helping out in disaster relief.

Check out ways your transferable skills can help grow your career:

Using Transferable Skills

- You **speak Spanish** at home, making you a good resource for the staff at work.
- As club treasurer you **managed the finances** with Excel. You know how to read a spreadsheet on department expenses.
- Your **marathon training experience** could help you relate to clients in a sports nutrition and wellness center.
- Another person took her skills as a **registered dietitian** and moved into a position in diabetic equipment sales
- Your experience **tutoring kids in math** may help you give a presentation to kids on healthy snack choices.
- Your experience as a **team leader in a fast-food job** can give you the ability to manage a group project.

Your skills are marketable and valuable. Employers are looking for people with the right skills and knowledge to do the job, both technical and soft skills. You need to know what skills you have and how you can use them to advance your career.

Identifying Your Skills

It's time to take an inventory to identify the skills, knowledge, abilities, and talents that can make you an asset to a company.

You've gained skills in many different ways:

- On the job
- In a classroom or training
- Family experiences
- Volunteering
- Memberships
- Sorority and Fraternity leadership
- Community involvement
- Hobbies
- Military service.

So, how do you identify the individual skills from each experience?
Look at:

- **job descriptions** - these list important skills and abilities needed to do each job. This can include jobs related to your volunteer experiences and interests.

- **course catalogs** - these list the skills and knowledge from a degree program

- **course syllabus** - an overview of skills learned in a class

- **training brochures** - identify key skills learned in a seminar or workshop

- **online job sites** - provide additional information about different careers

- **web sites and printed materials** - list the benefits of professional memberships and volunteering.

Your Career Planning Tool

The Career Planning Tool is a template file you can use to track your Skills, Knowledge, Abilities, Tools, and Technologies by key skill area, rare talents, and community service. Use this form to track your skills and identify work samples that show experience.The following skill types are listed on the form:

- Technical skills
- Soft skills
- Transferable skills
- Certification
- Tools & technologies
- Systems skills
- Resource management skills.

Access this template now to determine your key skill areas and begin to identify the types of skills that fall in each area. **You can also use this chart in Steps 2 and 4 to help you track your work samples and assemble your career portfolio.**

Template

Download the **Career Planning Tool** document template to help you track your skills and work samples within key areas.

By tracking and listing your skills, you will be able to decide which skills you want to promote to internship coordinators and employers with your career portfolio. At the same time you are collecting information, you will be creating your résumé.

Be sure to list all your experiences, whether they relate to dietetics or not. Transferable skills are sometimes the hardest to identify because you may do them in areas of your life where you aren't thinking about performing a job. As you create your list of life experiences, you will begin to identify your key skill areas.

Career Planning Tool

Planning for a Target Position: Use this sheet to identify your top three Key Skill Areas. Within each key skill area, indicate your skills, knowledge, and abilities along with the work samples you have to prove it, the skill type, source and the location of any electronic files. Use the following abbreviations when filling in skill types and source:

Skill Types: T= Technical, SS= Soft Skill, TR = Transferable Skill, T&T = Tools and Technology, Sp = Specialized Skill, C= Certification
Source: J= Job, E= Education, CS= Community Service, A= Activities, Mb= Professional memberships, M= Military, O= Other

Target Position:						Field:
Key Skill Area #1	Skills, Knowledge & Abilities	Work Sample	Skill Type	Source	Date	Source File Names/Location
Key Skill Area #2						
Key Skill Area #3						

Part 2- Identify Your Career Path

Managing Your Education

The field of dietetics has established clear guidelines for becoming a registered dietitian, so you are ahead in the career game compared to many other professions. **Here's the process to becoming a registered dietitian:**

1. Complete the minimum of a Bachelor's degree granted by a U.S. regionally accredited college or university, or foreign equivalent,

meeting the current minimum academic requirements for a Didactic Program in Dietetics accredited by ACEND®

2. Complete a 1,200 hour supervised practice program (internship) accredited by ACEND®

3. Successfully take the Registration Examination for Dietitians

4. Complete any state-required certification or licensing requirements

5. Continue education and recertification by compiling a Professional Development Portfolio (PDP) every 5 years.

Source: CDRNet.org

For dietitians, it's all about getting the right education, the right internship, and then continuing to learn and contribute to the field as a professional.

Most dietetic programs have very specific course plans and you should have much of your course calendar planned out. You may be in a didactic program where you get your degree and then apply for a dietetic internship. You might be in a combined program where the internship is integrated into the degree experience. It is very important to identify at the beginning of your program exactly what the requirements are and what you will need to do to get a dietetic internship. Begin collecting work samples and documenting your experiences as soon as possible throughout your undergraduate experience.

Take advantage of the career resources your school offers. Colleges and universities are being asked to prove that their students are being gainfully employed after receiving degrees, and they have an interest in helping you succeed. Meet with your counselor or adviser in your first year and map a course plan to make sure you take the classes you need in the correct order. Track your progress and make sure you have all the courses you need to graduate on time.

Dietetic Internships

To become a registered dietitian, you must graduate from an accredited program and participate in a Dietetic Internship (DI), generally lasting from 8 months to two years after gradua-tion. A DI requires 1200 hours in multiple areas of dietetic practice including clinical, community, and food service rotations. There are many different options for completing a dietetic internship, includ-ing part-time, full-time, distance programs with local rotations, com-pleting a graduate degree at the same time, or do an individualized supervised practice. Internships may focus on different aspects of the dietetic field, from general practice, to specialties in research, wellness, sports nutrition, and clinical practice.

A DI is required to become a dietitian, and it is a very competitive process. Twice a year, an electronic matching system connects stu-dent applicants to available dietetic internship openings. In 2013 5,444 dietetic students applied for internships, with around 2,900 available spots. That is approximately a 50% match rate. It may take a student several tries to get an internship match.

Start planning ahead for your DI at the beginning of your education. Most internships require a minimum GPA of 3.0, so your academic record is critical. You are also expected to show through your other experiences just why you are the right match for a specific intern-ship experience. Volunteer experiences, projects, presentations, articles, letters of recommendation and your application letter are critical to being chosen. You will use your career portfolio to docu-ment and track all your experiences.

Gain Experience

With only 50% of new graduates getting a dietetic internship, you should have other options available after graduation. Identify jobs that will build experience you can use for the next time you apply for an internship. Decide if you want to go on for additional education, and look for additional volunteer opportunities where you can hone your experience.

Building Your Career - Specialties and Certifications

Your education doesn't stop once you become an RD. You'll continue to learn on and off the job. As part of your continued certification, you will be required to complete a Professional Development Portfolio (PDP) on a five-year cycle. You will create your own learning plan based on your current job and future career goals, and then document your experiences and progress towards these goals. RDs are required to submit 75 CEU (Continuing Education Unit) credits and Dietetic Technicians (Registered) are required to submit 50 CEUs over the five year period.

There are many opportunities to expand your credentials and build your knowledge base, from becoming a board specialist in Oncology, Renal, Sports Medicine, or Pediatric Nutrition, or becoming a certified Diabetes Educator. Your career portfolio continues to help you document your achievements for promotions and new career opportunities.

Part 3- Create Your Career Plan

Skill Gaps - What's Missing and How Do I Know?

Now that you know your current skills and you've taken a look at the job you really want, it's time to identify the gaps. What additional KSAs and experiences do you need to get this job? Do you need a degree, certification, more experience or training, and how are you going to get it? Look at what you have, what you need, and then find the gaps. Then make a plan for getting the education, training, or experience you need to move ahead. You'll also want to set some career goals because YOU are in charge of your career, no one else.

- You know your current skills, now **identify the skills and experiences you still need** to do your target job position.

- Take a look at the **job descriptions, experience needed**, and **abilities of the people in that job.**

- Your **skill gap** is the difference in skills and experience between the two places.

- **Compare a generic job description and a job posting for a specific company.** Is there anything different between the two? Is the company looking for special skills? Keep this in mind when doing your gap analysis.

- **Your gap analysis prepares you to set your career goals.** Once you know the gap, make your plans to close the gap in the shortest amount of time.

Using GAP for a Specialty in Sports Nutrition

You've just gotten your first job as an RD in a health center. You really want to focus on sports nutrition and eventually would like to work with college athletes and get a Board Certification in Sports Nutrition. Since the certification requires you to have practiced for two years as a certified RD, plus work 1500 hours of practice in this specialty area, you have a number of options. Getting a master degree in Sports Nutrition would give you 1200 hours towards your certification. You could volunteer with a local high school team to develop training menus or work part time as a nutrition coach at the local gym. Developing a new sports nutrition bar, publishing your research and giving a presentation at a national conference would also add towards the hours you need. Start a consulting business focusing on sports nutrition and write a book. Identify the gaps between where you are now and where you want to be...then start planning.

Go back to the Career Planning tool template you've been using and identify the skills and experience you still need for your ideal job.

 Template

Download the **Career Planning Tool** document template to help you track your skills and work samples within key areas.

Set Your Career Goals

Once you've made some decisions on how you will get to your target job, you need to set some goals. **Goals** are performance achievements you set for yourself over a 2-5 year period. Break down your plan into a timeline. What do you need to do first? What can you be working on at the same time? Write your goal statements by including each component in the SMART rules:

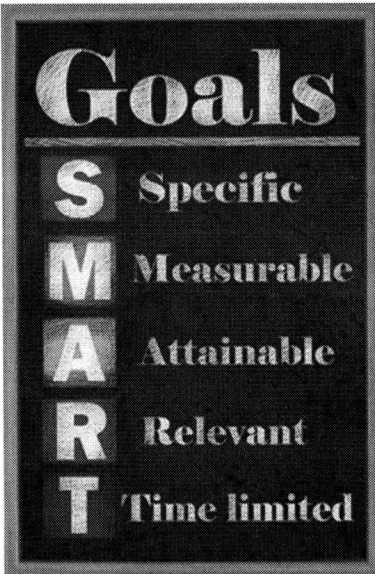

Specific– What are you going to do? - Be very detailed and clear.

Measurable– How will you know when you've reached the goal?

Achievable– How will you reach this goal? Your goal is possible for you to meet.

Realistic– You can achieve it within a set time period, It's do-able.

Time-based– When do you plan on reaching this goal? You have a set time frame for achieving this goal.

Here are some good rules for setting career goals:

- **Break down big goals**– having a series of smaller goals will be easier to reach and give you a sense of accomplishment when you meet each goal.

Big Goal:

- To get a masters degree in Dietetics with a specialty in Pediatric Nutrition by June 2017
- To start a consulting business on food allergies with children by September 2016.

Smaller Goals:

- To expand my food allergy blog site and newsletter following to 3,000 people by June 2016
- To teach an online class on food allergies by October 31, 2015.

- **Plan your goals for two to three years from now**– If you are in school, think about the education your need to have and anything you can do to gain skills and experiences. If you are starting in an entry-level position, think about the job you want to be doing in two to three years.

- **Make your goals broad enough to show that you are versatile**– Very specific goals can imply a narrow interest in the industry or in a specific job.

- **Write three to five goals**– If you only write one or two goals, you may appear unfocused and give the impression you're not really interested in advancing your career.

- **Keep your goals professional**– Make sure you focus on career goals rather than personal goals.

You should include a copy of your career goals in your career portfolio. Interviewers look at your goals and see if you fit the position and the culture of the company. They can also use your goals to identify the amount of additional training you may need to do the job.

Here is a list of goals appropriate for a college junior:

Two Year Goals:

- To maintain at least a 3.6 grade point average and get a dietetic internship in May 2017.
- To volunteer five hours per week at the local health clinic.
- To maintain a student membership in the Academy of Nutrition and Dietetics through May 2017.
- To take an online class on Nutritionist Pro™ by January, 2016.

Template

Download the Career Goals template, and use it as a starting point for developing your own goals.

Planning an Academic Program

It's your responsibility to keep track of the courses you need to graduate with your degree. **Meet with your school adviser** in your first year to map out your course plan, and then meet each semester to review your plan and make sure you are on the right track for graduating.

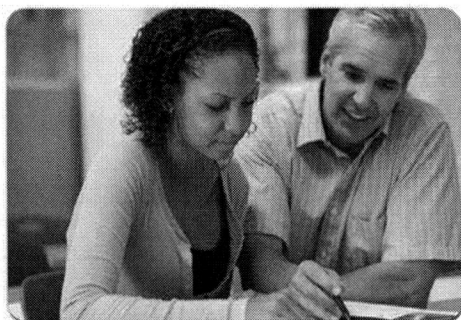

Many courses have prerequisites, those courses you have to take first before you can take a more advanced class. Spanish I would be a prerequisite for Spanish II. A course planner can help you keep track of the classes that are required and when you should take them in your school career. College course catalogs are your first source for identifying the classes needed for a particular degree.

Use the **Academic Planner tool** in the Templates section to help you set up and track your school course schedule. You will want to track:

- required courses for graduation.
- prerequisite courses and suggested timing for specific courses.
- number of credits for each class.
- electives required to meet minor or double major requirements.

 Template

Access the **Academic Planner Tool** in the templates section to help you track your skills and work samples within each course.

Course Tracking Tool

Check out the **Course Tracking Tool** template, designed to help you track the specific skills you are gaining from each of your classes.

Access the Template Forms and complete this form when you receive your class syllabus (an overview of the class.) Use it throughout the semester to track the knowledge and skills you are gaining from each class, as well as any class projects or assignments that could be used for work samples in your career portfolio. **The following types of information are tracked in the form:**

- Key skill areas.
- Work samples.

- Specific skills related to your major or degree area including the KRD area and competencies.
- Transferable skills.
- The grading scale.

 Template

Access the **Course Tracking Tool** in the templates section to help you track your skills and work samples within each course.

Course Tracking Tool

Complete a separate sheet for each class. Review your class syllabus at the beginning of the semester and begin filling in this sheet. Review it periodically through the semester and update information as needed. Use the Source File Names/Location column to keep track of any electronic documents that could be used as work samples.

Course:				Semester: Subject Area:	
Date	Project/ Assignment	Skills Demonstrated	Key Skill Area	Skill Type (Hard, Soft, Transferable)	Source File Names/Location

Capture Your Work Philosophy

You've chosen a career in the dietetic field, and it's time to show your enthusiasm and passion through your work philosophy. A **work philosophy** is a statement of your beliefs about yourself, people, and your outlook on life in your industry. It may also be called a management philosophy. This statement goes at the beginning of your Career Portfolio and gives the reader insight into you as a person. **Your work philosophy sets the tone for your career portfolio.** Take time to capture the things that you believe relate to dietetics. How do you feel about work? About this career? What do you believe about yourself and the work you'll be doing? Why do you want to do this work?

Here's the work philosophy of a graduating dietitian:

Work Philosophy

- A healthy lifestyle is a choice, and I need to live that choice for myself as an example to others.
- Being able to communicate the message to the client is key to impacting change.
- I want to be part of a winning health-care team.
- I believe in constantly learning and embracing new ideas and technology.

So, what does this statement tell an interviewer?

Here is a person who:

- **could be a good worker** who pays attention to detail.
- **wants to continue learning and growing their skills** on the job.
- **is looking for variety in their work–** they want to be doing different things.
- **wants to grow their career–** but also has personal goals.
- **wants to feel that their contribution and efforts to the company matter.**
- **is a self-starter,** someone who can think on their own and doesn't have to wait to be told what to do.
- **is looking to work in a company that is innovative, efficient, provides training and advancement opportunities,** where good work is rewarded.

Your work philosophy also helps you set standards for the kind of company where YOU want to work. Learn more about the company and see if it will be a good fit for you!

Here are some key things to think about when writing your own work philosophy:

- **Use bullet points** to make a concise statement.
- **Include 3-7 statements,** placing your most important beliefs first.
- **Ask a friend for their input.** They often have insights about you that come to mind immediately. Things that are such a part of you that you don't think about it.
- **Have your friend review it for clarity**- not approval.
- **Your work philosophy is never right or wrong**- it represents your key beliefs and values.
- **When do you know you've done a good job?** Write down what it looks and feels like.

Template

Download the Work Philosophy template, and use it as a starting point for developing your own work philosophy.

Prep Now

Wow, there's a lot to do in this step!

- Start tracking your skills and abilities with the Career Planning Tool.
- Identify your target job and do a Gap analysis.
- Set your goals to reach your target job.
- Fill out your course plan with the Academic Planning Tool.
- Use the Coursework Tracking Tool to track skills and samples. you can use from your classes.
- Write your work philosophy.

STEP 2: COLLECT AND ORGANIZE WORK SAMPLES

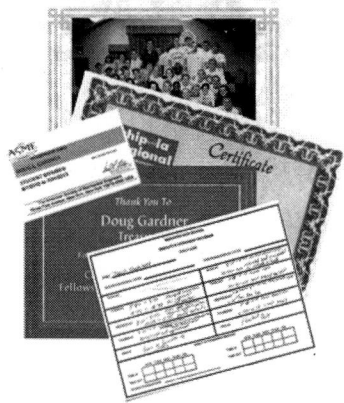

What Are Work Samples?

In Step 1, you created a detailed list of all your skills. Now look back at those skills and ask yourself this question:

What could I show to a person in an interview that proves I have these skills?

We use the term **work samples** to refer to *any* items you use to prove your skills and abilities, not just samples from a job. Some ePortfolio programs will use the term *artifacts* to mean the same thing.

Your work samples are unique to you, so they are powerful tools in your career portfolio. Work samples tell a story about who you are and what you've done. Your work samples set you apart.

You want to create a career portfolio that helps you talk about yourself in an interview setting. You should be able to show samples of your work, pictures that talk about your volunteer experiences, etc...

Each work sample should answer a question, prove a skill, or show why you are the right person.

Let's suppose you listed public speaking as one of your technical skills. How would you prove to someone you can speak in front of an audience? You could show:

- **a segment of a video** presentation.
- **a picture** of yourself speaking at a meeting.
- **copies of evaluations** showing positive comments about your speaking.
- **the slide deck** of a presentation on food allergies.
- **a letter from the teacher** who taught your public speaking class.
- **the skill listed** on your résumé.

The point is, you can use lots of things to prove you have a talent at public speaking.

What Makes a Good Work Sample?

There are a lot of work samples you could use to show that you are a good public speaker, but which of these would be the *best* sample to put into your career portfolio?

It depends... what's the purpose of your career portfolio?

- If you are applying for a summer job doing data entry, you may not need to include any samples. It's not a skill relevant to the job, but the sample could be used to show you have communication skills and you are probably a good team player.
- If you are applying for a job where you are doing training and patient education, you would definitely include one or more of the samples. The video and slide deck would be best, including the evaluations and letter from the teacher would give more

proof. These would show that you have the skills the employer is looking for in the position.

It gets a little trickier to identify and prove your soft skills, like customer service or time management. How do you *prove* you're a good multi-tasker? You may need to show:

- a **list of accomplishments** or goals you achieved on the job
- portions of a **job evaluation**
- a **letter from a club sponsor** thanking you for your excellent work introducing speakers at the local dietetic meeting last month, while you were studying for midterms and working a part-time job.

Is This A Good Work Sample? Ask Yourself...

- Does this sample demonstrate my skills?
- Does it show me in a positive way?
- Is it interesting to look at or boring?
- Can I explain the details of this sample?
- Is this sample relevant?

The answer to the last question, "Is this sample relevant?" may be yes or no, depending on what you are trying to show through the sample. So, make your motto: **"Collect Now... Sort Later."** It's better to save all your work samples now, and then decide if you want to use it when you are ready to actually assemble your career portfolio. We'll tell you from experience, when you decide you'll never need that report, or you are tossing out that research project on healthy snacks because you did it in high school, that's the sample you'll want later. We'll look at how to organize and save your samples later in this step.

The power of the career portfolio is your ability to customize it for different people and different uses. You need to be able to classify your work samples into different categories and group your samples together in a way that supports the skills you want to promote.

Customize your career portfolio for EVERY use!

Types of Work Samples

"Work" samples don't have to be only things you do on the job. They can be found in all areas of your life. A good work sample will prove your skills or help you talk about your experiences. Here are some of the types of work samples you can use in your career portfolio:

Documents

- Reports
- Projects
- Presentations
- Samples from your job
- Certificates
- Membership cards
- Awards
- Diplomas
- Course descriptions
- Plan of study
- Menus
- Dietetic case studies
- Certification requirements.

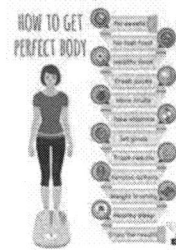

Something you have created

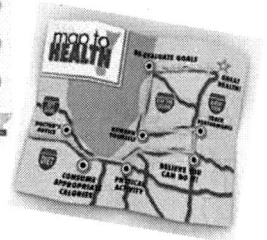

Membership Cards

Photos

- Show group work
- Projects
- Activities and interests
- Volunteer projects
- Internships
- 3-D projects or posters too big for the career portfolio.

Video and Audio files

- Presentations
- Training shorts
- Documentation
- Performing a task or skill
- Samples of Web sites or media created.

Letters that Recommend You to Others

- Recommendations
- Appreciation
- Customer service feedback
- Thank-you letters or cards
- Committee participation
- References
- Rotation evaluations
- Scholarship awarded
- Attendance/ participation.

Certificates & awards

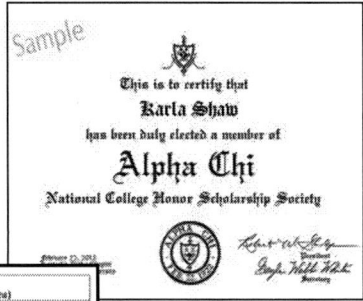

Documents you use on the job

Pictures, video, & audio

Recommendation letters

So, start collecting everything you've done, every certificate, every report or project, picture, or program brochure. Start a tote box or file folder and begin to gather your samples. Scan those documents electronically, and then set up new directories on your computer. Start copying projects, assignments, work documents, and media files you've created to your career portfolio directory.

> **Your New Motto is:**
>
> **Collect Now, Sort Later**

Be sure to scan any original certificates and awards, and then print a hard copy of the document. **Never include your originals in your career portfolio!**

Not everything you have will be used as a work sample in your career portfolio, but it's important to start collecting now.

Where to Find Work Samples

For some people, the biggest challenge of putting together a career portfolio is finding the samples. Sometimes you'll have samples of work you've created. For other skills you may have to ask for a letter of recommendation or create your own work samples. There are two categories of work samples: those you create or collect, and samples based on other people's views about you. **You'll find your work samples in the same places you found your skills and abilities in Step 1.** You'll look at your:

- schoolwork
- jobs
- community service
- extra-curricular activities, hobbies, and interests
- military experiences.

Academic Samples

Samples You Create or Collect

- Research papers
- PowerPoint presentations
- Special projects
- Course descriptions
- Overview of major/minor plans of study
- Program overviews
- Menus created with nutrition software
- Photos of you interacting with others
- Brief multimedia project summaries
- Copies of degrees received

Others Views About You

- Letter of recommendation
- Letter of introduction
- Scholarship letters
- Skill sets
- Reviews - Grading comments
- Thank you letters
- Rotation evaluations
- Speaking evaluations

To Do Now:

- **Start saving copies** of projects, presentations, and assignments.
- Keep a copy of the **course overview or syllabus** you receive at the beginning of the class.
- Keep a copy of the **course program booklet** from your school that describes all the classes and degree or training programs available.
- **Create your own skill list** - tracking skills you learned in the class and have your instructor sign-off on your ability to do the skill.
- Consider asking your teacher for a **letter of recommendation.**

Job Samples

Samples You Create or Collect

- Programs or systems
- Campaigns
- Marketing materials
- Job projects such as employee newsletters
- Special events
- Multimedia presentations
- Forms used on a regular basis
- Documents you have created to be more efficient
- Photos of you interacting with clients (if appropriate)
- Departmental operating procedures
- Highlights of responsibilities

Others Views About You

- Letter of recommendation
- Letter of introduction
- Thank you letters
- Skill sets
- Evaluations

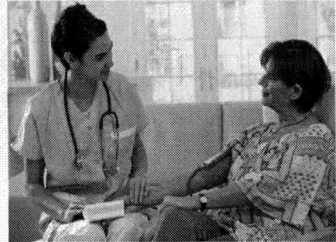

To Do Now:

- **Look at the tasks you do on a daily basis** - do you complete forms, do calculations, produce documents, write reports, write a review of equipment, or interact with people? Use samples to show your skills- but **be sure not to share confidential information.** Show a blank form instead of a completed form.
- **Create your own skill set list** - make a list of the skills you have on the job and have your employer sign off on your ability to do them.
- **Ask for a letter of recommendation** from your boss.
- **Keep thank you letters** from customers and coworkers.
- **Have someone take your picture** showing you working at your job using the equipment, talking to people, interacting. (Make sure you have people's permission to include their picture.)

Dietetic Internship Samples

Samples You Create or Collect

- Job responsibilities in each area
- An overview of the jobs you did in each rotation and what you learned.
- An overview of projects you were involved with
- Forms used on a regular basis
- Documents you have created to be more efficient
- Photos of you interacting with clients (if appropriate)
- Highlights of responsibilities from job description

Others Views About You

- Letter of recommendation
- Letter of introduction
- Thank you letters
- Skill sets
- Evaluations

To Do Now:

- Keep track of all your **evaluations and summaries** you create for each area of your internship.
- **Look at the tasks you do on a daily basis.** Use samples to show your skills- but **be sure not to share confidential information.** Show a blank form instead of a completed form.
- **Create your own skill set list.** Make a list of the skills you have used in various areas on the job and have your supervisor sign off on your ability to do them.
- **Ask for a letter of recommendation** from your supervisor and internship coordinator.
- **Keep thank you letters** from customers and coworkers.
- **Have someone take your picture** showing you working at your job... (Make sure you have people's permission to include their picture.)

Community Service Samples

Samples You Create or Collect

- Certificates
- Letters
- Photos
- Newspaper articles
- Media
- Plaques/Pins
- Thank you letters/cards
- Awards
- Recognitions

Others Views About You

- Letter of recommendation
- Letter of introduction
- Letter documenting volunteer hours
- Thank you letters
- Skill set sign-off
- Awards received

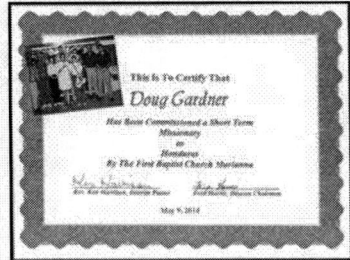

This Is To Certify That
Doug Gardner

May 9, 2014

To Do Now:

- **If you're looking for experience or want to document a group of skills, go to an organization and offer your services free of charge.** Start a project and see it through to the end.

- **Be sure to make it clear that all you want is a letter** documenting your time and skills. Then have some fun and test drive, develop, or refine your skills.

- **Offer the skills you feel you need help documenting.** You can use community service as a way of building your skills and proving your abilities.

- **Dietetic internship candidates use community service to build their experience.** Dietetic coordinators know that individuals who volunteer will be willing to stay a little longer to get the project done. It signals an individual who is interested in giving back to the community and the organization.

Community Service Projects

Community service is an important part of building skills and gaining experience to compete for dietetic internships and job opportunities. If there is a particular skill you want to improve, find an organization that needs help in that area, and volunteer! Volunteerism is a way to show your commitment to the dietetic profession and build your skills in a practical way. Join your local Academy and contribute to the website or write guest articles. Create a healthy food video and post it on YouTube™, teach a course in healthy cooking for a local continuing education program. Look for ways you can demonstrate your clinical skills, food service, and community experience.

There are several different types of organizations you can look to when volunteering:

- **Community Centered–** A volunteer activity designed to provide service in the local community. You can teach healthy snacking to school kids, organize a food drive, work in a community garden, or as an aid or diet tech in a nursing home, hospital, or daycare facility.

- **Service Organization–** An organization that exists or has a primary mission to provide community service. Examples include: Best Buddies, Habitat for Humanity, Special Olympics, Blue Key Society. Develop your leadership skills and soft skills.

- **Civic / Government–** Providing service in a capacity to a governmental function or office, especially when in training for leadership. Get involved in public policy activities or help with nutrition education programs for low-income participants.

- **Faith-Based–** Volunteering and providing a service that delivers an end product or an end goal for the community via a faith-based organization. Work at the local food bank, develop handouts on making healthy food choices or prepare meals for shut-ins.

- **Community Agency–** Organizations designed to provide service to the community at large. They have a formal volunteer structure in place. **Examples:** United Way, Red Cross, Special Olympics, Eli Lilly Foundation. Give presentations at local

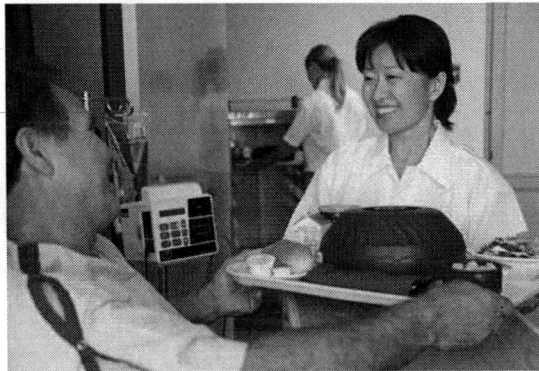

Employers like people who volunteer. When given a choice between two qualified candidates, employers will often choose the person who is actively involved in community service activities.

meetings, volunteer to prepare meals in crisis situations, or develop a special diet for runners preparing for a marathon. **Document your experiences and track them in your career portfolio.** Ask for a letter from the organization showing what work you have done, including the number of hours of service, and any particular skills you used.

Extracurricular Activities and Interests Samples

Samples You Create or Collect

- Membership cards
- Rosters
- Certificates
- Programs
- Presentations
- Pictures of you in action
- Blogs and articles
- Web pages
- Awards received

Others Views About You

- Letter of recommendation
- Letter of introduction
- Skill set sign-off
- Thank you letters
- Newspaper articles

Thank You To
Doug Gardner
Treasurer
For your outstanding leadership
Chipola Junior College
Fellowship of Christian Athletes
2011-2012

To Do Now:

Another place to look for skills and work samples is from your extra-curricular activities, hobbies, clubs, and social organizations.

- **Participation in extracurricular activities looks good on internship and job applications.** It shows people that you are well-rounded and responsible.
- **You can have fun learning new skills,** and it is well known that people who are involved in activities outside of school tend to do better academically.
- **Participation in sports and clubs can show soft skills** such as teamwork, problem-solving, time management, dedication, etc...
- **Take pictures of yourself in action** - team photos, volunteering, receiving an award, making a presentation, etc...

Be Aware of Confidential Information

If you are looking for work samples at your job, be sure you don't include samples with confidential information.

Samples should NOT include:

- personal information.
- customer information.
- company financial information.
- confidential workings of the company.

Carelessly displaying private and confidential information about another company raises huge questions about your reliability and personal ethics.

Consider the following guidelines:

- Never include confidential information.
- Get permission from individuals or companies before using a document.
- Before using a questionable work sample, ask yourself: What would I think if I saw this in someone else's portfolio? Would I be concerned about their integrity?

If in doubt, throw it out!

Collecting Good Work Samples

Your career portfolio needs to look professional, so make sure your work samples are clean, sharp, and easy to read. You want your career portfolio to look good, your images and printed pages to be clear and easy to read. A hard copy portfolio should have documents that are clear and sharp. Your ePortfolio should include images that are clear and load quickly. It's awkward being in an interview, wanting to show a sample on your tablet, and then having the image take forever to load. Take the time to scan your hard copy documents and clean up your images in a photo imaging software. You want your documents to look good, whether you are displaying copies of certificates and awards, taking photos of a project, or capturing a selfie of yourself and co-workers working at the food bank.

- **Make copies of all your printed certificates, awards, and documents.** If the documents are in color, make color copies. Make sure copies are centered and clean. Keep your original hard copy documents safe and include only high quality copies in your hard copy career portfolio.

- **Save documents at a higher resolution** so they will be clear when printed or viewed.

- To convert print documents to electronic, **use a good scanner** and make sure copies are centered and clean.

Capturing Work Samples with Mobile Devices

If you don't have access to a scanner, you can do great things with your cell phone and tablet.

Taking Photos with Impact

No one likes to look at photo albums with boring pictures, and your career portfolio should be the same. Any photos you include in your career portfolio should tell a story, whether you are demonstrating a skill, interacting with other people, or documenting your community service.

Remember these tips when capturing yourself in action:

- **Use good light,** try to use natural light instead of the built in flash of the camera.

- **Stage your photos** – Think about what you want to show in the shot, and the more interaction you have going on the better. Lighten up and try not to be so serious!

- **Take your photos at the highest resolution** and image quality. They will look better, especially when printed.

- If you're taking a selfie, **plan your background.** Make sure you can talk about the end picture.

- **Know your best side** - We all have a good side, so take your picture from that side. To make your face look slimmer, shoot your selfie from slightly above. If you're including your torso in the shot, turn one shoulder slightly toward the camera. Stick your neck out just a little to eliminate a bulge under your chin.

Capturing Documents With your Phone or Tablet

If you have hard copy documents that need to be converted to electronic copy, you will get the best results by using a flatbed scanner or a multi-use printer/scanner/copier set to a high resolution of 300 dpi or above. You can use the camera on your phone or tablet to capture the document, but you will have to take more steps to make sure that your images are high quality.

- **Use good lighting** – The better the lighting, the clearer the image.

- **Get as close as you can** to the document while capturing the whole image.

- **Take pictures of documents straight on**, not an angle which can leave parts of the document out of focus.

- **Take documents out of plastic sheet protectors** before taking the picture. This will eliminate reflections and the scan will turn out better.

- **Take shots at the highest resolution** or quality setting.

- **Avoid using the zoom** – When you zoom in, your image quality will be lower.

- **Keep the camera as still as possible.** Brace your hand or phone against a solid object. Hold still a little longer if there is a lag between pushing the button and snapping the photo.

- **Edit your images on your computer instead of your phone.** You'll have more options and can make sure that your images are clear and sharp.

Consider the Size and Quality of Your Images

You need to think about the size and quality of your documents when you take that first picture, or scan a document. Here are the basic rules:

- **Take your digital photos at the highest resolution - use the High quality or Fine setting.** They will be bigger in size, but the quality will be better. When you scan a document or take a digital photo, one of the settings you control is the **resolution** or **dpi** of the file. The resolution determines the quality of the image. The higher the dpi, the better the quality of the print.

- **Save your images and documents at a resolution of 300 dpi.** These produce a better quality printed page. When you look at the file in a photo editing program you may find that your pictures are saved at 72 dpi, but the size of the photo is also very large - often bigger than you could print on a sheet of paper. You can save these pictures to 300 dpi and then reduce the size of the picture to 6x4" and maintain the quality of your image for printing.

- **Save these same images at a resolution of 72 dpi for use in your ePortfolio.** A higher resolution image online makes for a bigger file, and a longer load time when viewing the image.

- **Set up your directories and label files to show if they are high or low resolution files.** When you create an ePortfolio and a hard copy career portfolio, you need to store your electronic documents at two different sizes. This means you will need to create two separate copies of the same file, one saved as a high quality document to be printed, and another smaller sized file for display on the screen.

General rules for file size:

- **Use 300 dpi images for print** – 300 dpi files are much larger and produce better quality print copy. A 72 dpi file can be grainy when printed to paper.

- **Use 72 dpi images for online viewing** – The 72 dpi file is smaller and optimized for displaying on the screen. The 300 dpi file is much larger, so it can take longer to load when displayed online. **Online files are usually saved in .jpg, .gif, or .png format.**

> **Resolution**
>
> **Use 300dpi for print.**
>
> **Use 72 dpi for online.**
>
> **Always capture images at the highest quality resolution.**
>
> **You can downsize and keep the quality, but your image will blur if you upsize from a lower quality image.**

- **Always scan or save your image at 300 dpi, then save a separate copy at 72 dpi** – you can size an image down to 72 dpi for viewing online, but if you try to take a 72 dpi file and save it as a 300 dpi file, you will always lose quality and the image will be blurry.

- **Think about the viewing size when saving 72 dpi images** – How big does your document need to be on screen? Do you want people to read the entire document in detail, or is a smaller copy of the sample good enough? The smaller the file size the faster the file will load on screen.

Requesting Letters of Support

A letter of support from employers, instructors, etc., can provide additional proof of your abilities. Letters provide personal references from people who have seen your performance. You may need to rely more on letters of recommendation when you don't have many work samples, or when the type of work you do doesn't generate as many physical samples.

You should ask for letters from people who know you and/or your work personally. Instructors, supervisors, owners, mentors, pastors, volunteer coordinators... all can be appropriate references. You should be proud to be associated with these people. If you don't like them, they probably don't like you, and you don't want a letter from them.

Types of Support Letters

Letter of Recommendation– This letter highlights your skills, abilities, and character from the writer's personal experience with you, and serves as a testimonial to your good traits.

Letter Documenting Volunteer Hours– This letter focuses specifically on documenting community service participation. This may be a more impersonal letter just confirming the facts, or it could include more details about the skills and contributions you've made to the organization.

Asking for a Letter

- **Request your letter in advance**– before you need it. Allow 2-3 weeks to receive your letter. Ask for the letter while you are close to the event or you are still in contact with the person.

- **Be polite**– include please and thank you.

- **Give them guidelines**– Your letter needs to help guide the person writing the recommendation to focus his or her letter on key skills and areas of your personality that you want addressed. Begin by telling the person the purpose of the letter, then giving them a list of traits, skills, or attributes you want addressed. Here are some examples:

  - Leadership
  - Ability to work in groups
  - Ability to self-motivate
  - Ability to meet customer needs
  - Your work with diabetic patients

  - Your skills in working with social media
  - Ability to complete work
  - Ability to supervise
  - Management skills
  - Creativity
  - People skills.

  - ▲ **The letter should include background information on how they know you** and how long you have been associated with the organization or project.
  - ▲ **The letter should be on official letterhead**, should have an ink signature, and should not be folded.
  - ▲ The recommendation letter you receive should be **addressed as "Dear Future Employer."**
  - ▲ **Don't be afraid to proof their work.** If you find a mistake, be humble and ask for a correction.

Template

The following sample recommendation request letter is available in the template section. Use it as a starting point for writing your own letters. (**Recommendation request** document)

Inside Address

Today's date

Dear Professor Watkins:

I was a student of yours last term in your Advanced Medical Nutrition Therapy class. I earned an A in your class, and was an active participant every day so you probably remember me. I will be graduating in May, and I am currently working on assembling my career portfolio. Could you please write a letter of recommendation addressing the following skills:

- My ability to work in teams
- My ability to present findings professionally
- My ability to identify diet-related health problems
- My ability to recommend nutrient intakes.

It would also be helpful if you could indicate how long you have known me and on what occasions you have worked with me. I would appreciate it if you could address the letter to "Dear Future Employer" and leave the letter unfolded.

I would greatly appreciate receiving this letter within the next two weeks. Please call or e-mail me and let me know when it would be convenient for me to pick up the letter. Thank you very much for your consideration and all your help. Please feel free to call me if you have any questions.

Sincerely,

Russell Jackson

Russell Jackson

123 45th Ave.

Any State, NY 01011

(123) 456-7890 - Home phone

e-mail: rsljksn@provider.com

Creating a Skill Set

A **skill set** is a list of related skills and how well you can perform them. Skill competencies from your dietetic internship rotations are excellent samples to include in your career portfolio. Each set is signed off on by the internship director or preceptor.

Skill sets are not only a list of your abilities, but they can also show the level of your abilities. You can use a skill set to track your progress on achieving your goals and increasing your skill levels. Check out the template section for a form you can use to create your own skill set. **This skill set measures ability at three levels:**

Awareness— You have awareness of the knowledge/skill, and have completed the task at least once.

Practicing— You are able to follow a guide to complete a task.

Mastery— You are able to consistently perform the task without effort.

Have your instructor or employer sign off on your current level of ability. As you improve your skills, you can have them sign off on higher levels of achievement, showing your progress.

Here's a skill set created to track food handling and preparation:

Food Handling and Preparation

Awareness	Practicing	Mastery
Has awareness of the knowledge/skill, and/or has completed the task at least once.	Is able to follow a guide to complete the task.	Is able to consistently perform the task without effort.

Is able to develop a low-sodium diet.

print name	print name	print name
signature	signature	signature
date	date	date

Is able to establish a specialized patient diet.

print name	print name	print name
signature	signature	signature
date	date	date

Is able to prepare and update tray cards.

print name	print name	print name
signature	signature	signature
date	date	date

Creating Your Own Skill Sets

It's easy to create your own skill sets:

- **Look at your job description to identify skills you want to show.**
  Shop through the job requirements and evaluate your skills against the list. If you don't have a job description, go online and search for one to use.

Now expand and refine this list of skills...

- **List the things you have done on the job–** Take a look at an average day at work, and list the things you do. Consider both your technical skills and soft skills. Be specific - you may be thinking "I'm just working with people to prepare food for patients, but actually you're also responsible for sanitation, flow of the tray line, and making sure the meal is balanced to the specific needs of each patient. We often forget all the skills and tasks we do in a day.

- **List unique skills.** Focus on your creative skills, your problem-solving skills, and your ability to do several things at once. Focus on your patient education skills, your problem-solving skills, or your unique knowledge and experience as a diabetic.

Template

A blank skill set template is available to download. Use it as a starting point for creating your own skill sets. (Skillset.doc)

Career Smarts

Get A Head Start... Create your skill sets while still in school. Take time at the beginning of each term or rotation to review the skills and competencies you expect to achieve in each course. Use the *Course Tracking Tool* template to track the skills you're learning.

Organizing Work Samples

It's important to set up a good organization system to track your work samples at the beginning of the Career Portfolio process. Being able to easily and quickly access your work samples will make it much easier to assemble and customize your career portfolio as you collect more and more work samples. Your work samples are generally going to be a collection of:

- Hard copies and originals (awards, certificates, letters, cards, physical products created, programs, etc.)
- Electronic files (documents, videos, audio files, and graphics.)

Start a tote box or file folder to keep track of your hard copy originals. You will want to scan those documents and store them electronically on your computer. When you want to use the document in a hard copy portfolio, print the document and include it in your career portfolio.

Never include your originals in your career portfolio!

Set up a new directory on your computer called Career Portfolio, and then create sub-directories to track your electronic samples. Start copying those projects, assignments, work documents, and media files you've created over to your career portfolio directory.

Filing Electronically

Many of your work samples will be generated from electronic files, so it's important to get your computer files organized at the beginning. You need to set up a good system of directories and sub-directories, and then figure out a consistent way of naming each file so you can quickly identify its contents.

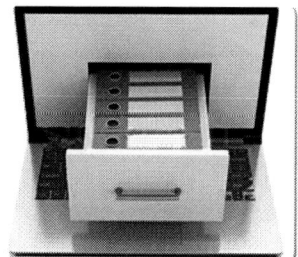

The most important rule to creating a filing system is to keep it simple. If you create too many categories, you can spend more time trying to figure out where your sample fits, or trying to remember where it was filed. **The second important rule is to use a system that**

works for you. What makes sense to one person can be totally useless to someone else. Use the suggestions here as a guideline and starting place for getting organized.

Begin by creating a new directory on your computer just for your work samples, then create your sub-directories to store the files. The most common way to sort work samples is by the *source* of the work sample such as:

- Job / Work
- Education / School
- Community Service
- Activities / Extracurricular.

Within these directories you can add additional directories that track the type of information stored in the files. A breakdown might look like this:

- Job / Work
  - ▲ Projects
  - ▲ Evaluations
  - ▲ Letters
  - ▲ Certificates.
- Education/School
  - ▲ Class 1 samples
  - ▲ Class 2 samples
  - ▲ Certificates/ Awards.
- Community Service
  - ▲ Organization 1
  - ▲ Organization 2, etc.....

> **Remember:**
>
> **Keep it Simple**
>
> **Use a system that works for you**

You might choose to organize your samples by the key skills they represent. Keep in mind that some of your samples may show multiple skills and could appear in different key area sections.

Use the Career Planning and Course Tracking Templates– If you've been using the Career Planning tool and the Course Tracking templates introduced in Step 1, you should have a good idea of where your samples came from and what skills they represent. There is also a column for identifying where the file is stored. Use this template as your index so you can quickly find any sample you need.

Naming Your Electronic Files

Now that you have a place to put all those samples, what do you name the samples? This makes a big difference. If you know what you are looking for and it has a proper name it is a lot easier to find. Let's look at some simple rules to follow to keep your electronic documents named for locating. After all what's the point in storing all this information if you can't find it?

Example:

- Part one: source
- Part two: type of sample
- Part three: keyword description
- Part four: month-year
- Part five: number of dpi saved.
  - 72
  - 300

Example:

cjc-academic-deans list 02-12 -300.tif

cjc-academic-deans-list-02-12-72.jpg

Follow this process for scanning and saving hard copy documents:

- Scan all originals and hard copies not already in electronic format.
- Save files at both 72 and 300 dpi.
- Save as source file and as PDF for documents.

- Copy to the appropriate folder.
- Save all original hard copies— only work from quality copies.
- Back up your directories.

Keeping Your Files Safe

Keep a backup copy of your files. You may want to store all your work samples on an cloud drive, external drive or USB drive. It's also a good idea to keep an extra backup copy at another location. Drives can fail, and you want to be sure you don't lose all your hard work!

Don't forget to make a backup copy!

Labeling Work Samples

Each work sample should have a label telling someone about the sample they are viewing. Your label should let the viewer understand what they are seeing without your help.

If you are creating a hard copy career portfolio, we suggest you create an **overview card** for each sample. You should be able to hand your portfolio to another person and they should be able to understand what each sample is and why it is in your portfolio.

The overview card should contain the following information about the work sample:

- Title
- Purpose of the sample
- Date developed
- If it was a group effort, include the names of the people who were involved
- List the skills shown by the sample in keyword format and include the related KRD skill area.

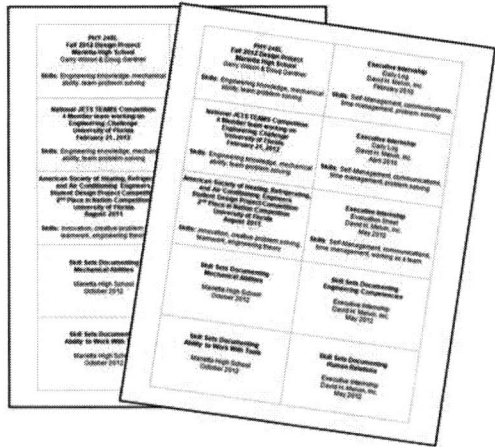

Template

You can download an work sample overview card template. You set up 10 cards to a page and print them out onto a blank sheet of business cards. Drop the individual card into the sheet protector holding the sample.

Some people wait until they are ready to assemble their portfolio to create their overview cards, but you might want to print them ahead and just attach the card to your sample with a paper clip.

Here's a sample overview card:

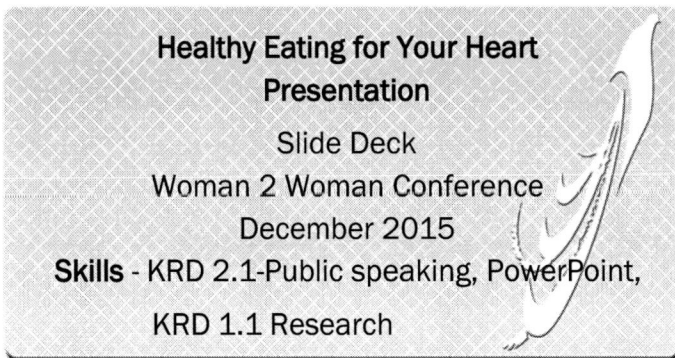

Healthy Eating for Your Heart Presentation

Slide Deck
Woman 2 Woman Conference
December 2015
Skills - KRD 2.1-Public speaking, PowerPoint,
KRD 1.1 Research

Make sure any work samples in your ePortfolio also have a descriptive label. You should be able to add a caption or description to each electronic sample. Follow the same rules as the Overview cards for your hard copy career portfolio. It's more than likely that anyone viewing a portion of your ePortfolio is doing it without you standing over their shoulder, so your work samples need to be self-explanatory.

> **Be sure to add a good label or description to each sample in your ePortfolio**

Prep Now!

Collecting work samples is an ongoing project!

- Start collecting work samples.
- Scan your hard copy documents and save your originals in a safe place.
- Set up a filing system for hard copy samples and electronic copies.
- Use the Career Planning Tool and Course Tracking Tool templates to track your skills and work samples.
- Request any letters of recommendation from employers, teachers, volunteer coordinators, etc.
- Create your own skill sets as needed.
- Create overview cards for each sample.

Step 3: Create Your Résumé and Your Online Presence

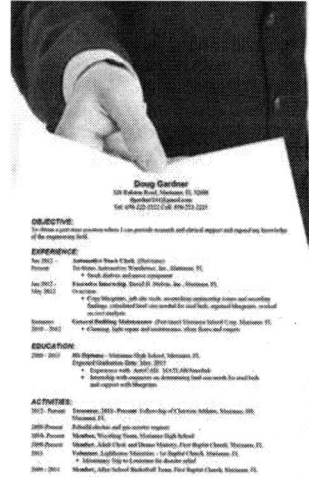

Setting Professional Standards

Dietitians are the ultimate professionals.
The Accreditation Council for Education in
Nutrition and Dietetics of the Academy of Nutrition and Dietetics
(ACEND®) has set the standards high to be in the dietetic profession. From the very first class in a didactic program, professionalism
is part of the education that every student receives. The concepts of
value, compassion, work ethic, commitment, communication, credibility, continued learning and education, and having a professional
attitude are all part of the program.

You cultivate your professional presence through your competencies, your communication, your attitude, your appearance, and your
credentials. In Step 3, we'll look at ways develop your online presence and create a résumé that will represent you as a professional.

Your résumé is the overview of your skills and
your experiences. While you may think a
résumé is only used when you want to get a
job, it really is an overview of your skills and
abilities and is also used when submitting your
qualifications for a dietetic internship and
scholarships. It's also the place to start when
creating a professional online presence.

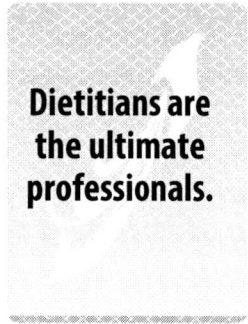

**Dietitians are
the ultimate
professionals.**

The Résumé: Your Big-Picture Overview

Once you've started collecting and categorizing your work samples, it will be easy to create a targeted résumé to help you get an interview. **A résumé is a written document that gives your employment background, education, and highlights your skills.** It is usually 1 to 2 pages long, and is used to summarize your skills. It's the standard practice to submit your résumé to an employer when you are applying for a job or internship. Employers use the résumé to sort out the people they want to interview for a position. We often say that **"Your résumé gets you an interview, and your career portfolio gets you the job."**

People use your résumé to see if:

- you have the skills they need.
- you fit their corporate culture.
- you will be able to help them save or make money.
- you have special skills that would be a bonus.
- they want to learn more about you through an interview.

Making the Cut

Your résumé has to make it through the screening process... For many jobs, a real person may not be reading your résumé at all. Many companies scan the résumés they receive and use software to do the first round of "yes or no" on applicants. They can enter specific word and terms and the program searches each résumé for those keywords. The more keywords on your résumé that connect, the more likely you are to get a call for an interview.

A recent study showed that many recruiters actually looked at a résumé for just 6 seconds! Recruiters scan for the basic information of name, current position, with company and dates, previous positions with company and dates, and education. Making your résumé clear and concise is critical to having your résumé make the cut.

So, how do you write a résumé that doesn't immediately go to the reject bin? Easy...

- Customize your résumé for each use.
- Use the right format to highlight your skills.
- Use the right keywords and language.
- Emphasize the skills they want to see.
- Use an eRésumé with hyperlinks to key work samples.
- write an eye-catching cover letter to send with your résumé.
- use social media along with your career portfolio and have a good Internet presence.

Different Résumés for Different Audiences

Your résumé is a resource you use to market yourself, and you need to have the right tool for the right occasion. You really should have at least three versions of your résumé:

1. The Stylized Résumé - This one looks good. It has a personalized look and feel. You send this one to set you apart from other résumés in a pile. This is the one you send directly to associate of a colleague you met on LinkedIn™, or you put into your hard copy career portfolio. It's the copy you print off and give to an interviewer to impress.

2. The eRésumé - This one still looks good, but it features live hyperlinks to your best work samples. One click, and the person can see the evaluation on your clinical rotation, the poster you created for the health fair, or watch part of the presentation you gave to the local 4-H group. This is the one you send to the internship coordinator when you want her to see your best work, the colleague you've met on LinkedIn™, or as an attachment to the thank you e-mail to the interviewer after you've had a phone interview.

3. **The Uploadable Résumé** - This is the résumé you use when you go online to a job bank or employer site and need to upload a copy of your résumé. This version of your résumé has very little formatting and is designed to be scanned and converted automatically by software into a standardized format. At the same time the software is reviewing the contents, looking at keywords, dates, and job titles, and starting to sort out your qualifications. This one doesn't look pretty, but it gets the job done. **Choose the right format** for your résumé based on your job history and education.

Using Keywords and Action Verbs

Keywords are terms that draw people into specific skills and abilities. When you do a search on the Internet, your are using keywords. Think about your résumé as if it were a Web site. What terms do you want people to look for and find?

You might see some of these keywords on the résumés in this section:

dietitian, clinical nutrition, wellness, and sports nutrition education, counselor, student athletes, coaching staff, 40 bed facility, diet analysis, food records, online blog, social media, portion control, healthy eating, health fairs, bariatric patients, allergy awareness, family resource center, Academy of Dietetics and Nutrition, treatment plans, student liaison, dietetic student

> ### Using Keywords
>
> **Not sure what keywords to use in your résumé?**
> Take a look at the job posting- What keywords do they use in the description?
>
> Go online and find a job description for a similar position - See what terms they use to describe the skills, work activities, tools and technology used on the job.

award, National College Honor Scholarship Society, Alpha Chi, scholarship award

The names of employers, schools and organizations, job titles, and degrees could also be important keywords depending on the company doing the hiring.

The more hits on keywords, the higher the possibility this résumé will appear on the list of people to interview.

Action verbs are used on a résumé to describe what you have done. People reading a résumé tend to look at the action verbs, while the computer scanning software looks at keywords. There is a detailed list of action verbs in the Resources section on pages 151-153.

Here are good action verbs to include in a résumé in this section:

develop, counsel, present, host, design, promote, assist, perform, analyze, coordinate, partner with, assess, document, maintain

Organizing Your Résumé

There are several ways of organizing a résumé depending on your experiences, skills, and target industry. These are the two most popular formats:

Chronological résumés– Information is organized by date. Information is listed with the most recent experiences first. This is the most common and straightforward résumé format. Use a chronological résumé when you have job experience relevant to the position for which you are applying and you want to emphasize your education and your experience. You can focus on the organizations you've worked for and your specific accomplishments in each job.

Functional/ Skill résumés– This type of résumé is designed to highlight accomplishments and specific skills. It is organized by the different kinds of skills you can perform, such as management skills, marketing, finance, etc.

Chronological Résumés are the most common format. Usually includes these sections:

- Contact Information
- Qualification Summary
- Work History
- Education
- Volunteerism/ Interests/ Activities / Awards.

Information in each section is organized by date, with the most recent listed first. If you have less work experience and more education, put your education section first.

Education- Include:

- School name
- School's city and state
- Dates attended
- Degree earned
- Major area of study
- Relevant projects.

List your current college education with expected graduation dates. List any certifications or additional training you've taken past high school.

You can include work experience, volunteer jobs, co-ops, and internships.

List your most recent job first.

Personal Data- Contact information including:

- Your name
- Address
- Phone number
- E-mail address.

Do not include information about your age, marital status or health. Do not include a photo.

Qualification Summary:

- 1-2 sentences about what you have to offer the employer. Customize for each employer.

Work Experience- Include:

- Job title
- Employer's name
- Employer's city and state
- Employment dates
- Responsibilities using keywords.

You can include work experience, volunteer jobs, co-ops, and internships.

List your most recent job first.

Activities/ Interests- Include:

- Volunteer experience
- Awards and certificates
- Extracurricular activities
- Professional memberships.

List activity, organizations, dates, positions held

Volunteer activities and member-ships may be listed under separate headings depending on how many activities and organizations you include.

Qualification Summary

Kelly Morgan

Personal Data

100 West Way• city, state, zip
Phone: (987) 654-3210 • Fax: (123) 456-7891 • E-Mail: kmorgan@provider.net

Qualifications
Future dietitian with a focus on clinical nutrition, wellness, and sports nutrition

Education

Education

Master of Science – University of Kentucky, Lexington, KY
Major: Nutrition and Food Science – Degree expected May 2017

Bachelor of Science - Murray State University   Murray, KY
Major: Nutrition and Food Science - Degree: May 2015
    Emphasis in clinical nutrition, wellness, and sports nutrition

Employment

Experience

Graduate Teaching Assistant, University of Kentucky, Lexington, KY
June 2015 - Present
- Assist professor in an Introductory Nutrition course.
- Helped develop two new courses on the use of social media and online counseling of patients.
- Provide sports nutrition education to student-athletes and c

Student Health Liaison, Murray State University, Murray Health Center.
September 2012 - May 2014
- Responsible for assisting students with health and wellness inquiries.
- Performed diet analysis on student three day food records.
- Assisted with various presentations, health fairs, promotions regarding nutrition and health related issues.
- Developed handouts, posters and bulletins for promoting health and wellness.
- Conducted presentations in student dormitories to promote low-fat living.

Honors & Awards
- Outstanding Dietetic Student Award, American Dietetic Association - June 2014
- National College Honor Scholarship Society Alpha Chi Member - 2013 - 2014
- Scholarship Award – Academy of Dietetics and Nutrition - June 2013

Memberships

Activities

- Academy of Dietetics and Nutrition (2011 - present)
- Kentucky Academy of Dietetics and Nutrition member (201
  - Student Liaison, 2013-2014
- American Culinary Federation (2010 - present)

Community Service
- Medical Nutrition Therapy for the Treatment of Overweight and Obesity – presentation for Northwestern Memorial Hospital Sleep Clinic - February 2015
- LifeHouse Care Center for Women, volunteer 2015
- Counselor in the Family Resource Center - Calloway County Schools - 2013-2014
- Presentation on allergy awareness to IL HeadStart Organization - April 2014

Community Service

Functional/ Skill Résumés are like a chronological résumé with skills from education and work experiences broken out as a separate section.

Usually includes these sections:

- Skill Sets
- Contact Information
- Qualifications Summary
- Work History
- Education
- Volunteerism/ Interests/ Activities / Awards.

Use a skill résumé when:

- You want to focus on your transferable skills rather than your work experience or education.
- You have fewer work experiences, or they aren't directly related to the position you want.
- You have gaps in your employment history.
- Your skills come from experiences not necessarily associated with a job or education.

The Functional or Skill résumé has an additional section called Skill Sets.

The key skill areas you chose for your career portfolio in Step 2 will be the same areas to promote in a functional résumé.

- In the skill résumé you pull the details from the Work Experience, Education, and Activities sections of the résumé and organize them by key skill area.
- Only the bare details are included in the work experience, education, and activities sections of the résumé.

The Résumé: Your Big-Picture Overview

Kelly Morgan

100 West Way• city, state, zip
Mobile: (987) 654-3210 • E-Mail: kmorgan@provider.net

Qualifications
Future registered dietitian with a focus on clinical nutrition, w **Skill Sets**

Skill Sets
Clinical Nutrition
- Counselor in the Family Resource Center - Calloway County Schools
- Provide sports nutrition education to student-athletes and coaching staff.
- Responsible for assisting students with health and wellness inquiries.
- Performed diet analysis on student three day food records.

Media and Wellness Promotion
- Course development on the use of social media for nutritional education and online counseling of patients
- Host of online blog: Power-Food.com, focused on healthy eating and portion control
- Presenter at health fairs, promoting nutrition and health related issues.
- Design and development of handouts, posters and bulletins for promoting health and wellness
- Conducted presentations in student dormitories to promote low-fat living.
- Presentation on allergy awareness to IL HeadStart Organization

Leadership
- Kentucky Academy of Nutrition and Dietetics member (2011 - present)
  - Student Liaison, 2013-2014
- Outstanding Dietetic Student Award, Academy of Nutrition and Dietetics - June 2014
- National College Honor Scholarship Society Alpha Chi Member - 2013 - 2014
- Scholarship Award – Academy of Nutrition and Dietetics - June 2013
- LifeHouse Care Center for Women, volunteer 2015

Education
Master of Science – University of Kentucky, Lexington, KY
Major: Nutrition and Food Science – Degree expected May 2017

Bachelor of Science - Murray State University   Murray, KY
Major: Nutrition and Food Science - Degree: May 2015
Emphasis in clinical nutrition, wellness, and sports nutrition

Employment
Graduate Teaching Assistant, University of Kentucky, Lexington, KY
June 2015 - Present

Student Health Liaison, Murray State University, Murray Health Center.
September 2012 - May 2014

Professional Career Portfolio Available

General Guidelines for Creating Your Résumé

- **Use the résumé templates found in Microsoft Word® as a starting place** to create your stylized résumé. There are many different versions to choose from and you can easily enter your information into the template.

- **Keep your résumé to 1-2 pages.**

- **Keep your résumé easy to read**– use basic 11- or 12-point fonts like Arial, Verdana, and Times New Roman.

- **Check your résumé for typos, formatting errors, and correct information.**

- **Target your résumé to the position you want:**
  - ▲ Customize your résumé for each target position– every time!
  - ▲ Use the right keywords which focus on key skills, job titles, and your rare talents

- **Let people know you have a career portfolio.** Add the following line to the bottom of your résumé:

  Professional Career Portfolio available for review

eRésumés

An **electronic résumé**, or **eRésumé**, is a résumé you design to look good when viewed in an e-mail message or on a web page. An eRésumé usually contain **hyperlinks** to work samples. When the link in the document is clicked, the sample will open in a separate window. **By showing your samples in your eRésumé you're giving the employer an extra look at your abilities.** Take a look at Karla's eRésumé on the next page. Each underlined phrase is a hyperlink to a work sample.

Karla Shaw

100 West Way Murray, KY 45334
kshaw440@mail.com
Mobile: (270) 654-2111

QUALIFICATIONS:

Sports nutritionist and future dietitian with a focus on educating individuals on how to control weight and develop general health with education and exercise.

EXPERIENCE:

Sept. 2015-
Present
Graduate Teaching Assistant (GTA) (Part-time)
University of Kentucky
Lexington, KY
Responsibilities:
- Assist professor with classroom management of two courses
  - Syllabus for NFS 301 - Introduction to Dietetics Course
  - Syllabus for NFS 512 – Professional Practice with Social Media
  - Assist professor with research and other duties as needed
- Grade homework and provide classroom support for students in a lab setting
- Experience using these software programs:
  - ValuSoft MasterCook
  - Gnutrition
  - Cybersoft Primero Software Suite
  - eTritionWare software
  - DietMaster Systems Clinical Nutrition

Aug 2012 -
May 2015
Student Health Liaison (Part-time)
Murray State University Health Center
Murray, KY
- Poster: Healthy Studying for Finals Week
- YouTube Video: Health Portions without the Measuring Cup
- Brochure: Nutrition Meet-Ups

Jan 2010 –
July 2011
Dietary Aide (Part-time)
Murray State Health Center
Murray, KY

EDUCATION:

Aug 2015-
Present
MS in Nutrition and Food Science
University of Kentucky, Lexington, KY
Expected Graduation – May 2017

Graduated
May 2015
BS in Nutrition and Food Science
Murray State University, Murray, KY
Achievements:
- Clinical Samples - Multiple Sclerosis

ACTIVITIES:

Jan 2012 -
Present
Member
Academy of Nutrition and Dietetics, Kentucky Chapter
Achievements:
- Student Liaison
- Poster: Healthy Studying for Finals Week
-

Jul 2012 - Jul
2012
Hugger, Special Olympics, Murray, KY
- Hugger - Special Olympics

Guidelines for eRésumés

Here are some general guidelines to follow when e-mailing a résumé:

- **Only link to relevant work samples.** If someone is going to take the time to click and view a sample, make sure it's worth their time and the sample is self-explanatory.

- **Save your résumé in a PDF format if possible.**

  - ▲ A PDF file cannot be edited or changed by anyone else, and your fonts and formatting will be intact.

  - ▲ To view the file, someone must have Adobe Acrobat Viewer™ loaded on their computer. The Acrobat Viewer™ can be downloaded online for free.

  - ▲ To create a PDF file you can use the full version of Adobe Acrobat™ or download another program - Google "PDF Creator" to find other programs that will help you create PDF files.

- **Use standard fonts such as Times New Roman, Arial, Tahoma, or Geneva when sending your résumé as a Word or text file.** If you do send your résumé in a Word format, the document may display differently on the recipient's computer than it does on yours. Using standard fonts will make sure it looks the way you want.

- **Test all hyperlinks** to be sure they are correct.

- **Name your document with your name, target position and date unless otherwise instructed in the application process.** Like this: Karla Shaw-Mar15-Internship.pdf

> **Only include links to your key samples**
>
> 🗝
>
> **People are not going to click on a link to view a sample unless something compels them.**

- **Keep your file size down to 2MB or less.** This shouldn't be a problem if you are just attaching your résumé or a cover letter. Some companies have firewalls that block large attachments.
- **Include a cover letter as an attachment or as the e-mail.** Cover letters are sent with the résumé and give the reader a brief introduction to who you are and the position you want. Let them know you have links to key samples in the attached résumé.
- **Put your contact information in the body of the e-mail.**

Uploadable Résumés

If you are applying for a job, you're probably filling out your application online and uploading your résumé to the company's website. If this is the case, you'll want to have a specially formatted version of your résumé ready to upload. The software on the site reads your résumé and automatically pulls out different information and puts it into a standardized résumé format. You usually have an option to review the résumé after you upload it, so you can correct any information that ended up in the wrong place. You can also use this résumé to cut and paste sections of your résumé into an online form. If your uploadable résumé is not formatted correctly, you may find yourself getting error messages while uploading your résumé, or having to spend a lot of time fixing the "automatic" placement of your information on the form.

Résumé Parsing...

When you upload your résumé in a very plain format to an online job site and software automatically extracts the information and puts it into a standardized résumé format. At the same time your résumé is analyzed for keywords, dates, and skills.

Here are the guidelines for creating an uploadable résumé:

Formatting

- Save your résumé in Microsoft Word format. Make sure your file has a .docx extension, not .doc

- Don't use any headers, footers, or page numbers

- Don't use graphics, icons, or Wingdings

- Don't use columns or tables in Microsoft Word or use a Word résumé template

- List information on separate lines like you were addressing a letter and left justify, don't center information.

- Write out dates like this: December 2015

Fonts

- Think plain – Arial, Courier, Calibri, Tahoma

- Don't use bullets, underline, or small caps or italic.

- Use only uppercase and bold to distinguish headings and key information.

Organizing Information

- List your contact information at the top

- Use standard résumé headings to separate each section, keep each section separate and don't combine sections

- Use tabs for formatting information, and list each piece on a separate line

- Keep all the information for a job together with single spacing. Separate each job with a blank line. Same goes for education.

- If you had more than one job at a company, treat it as if it were a totally separate company and job. Don't indent the jobs under one company.

- List the skills used on each job in a block format with the job information

Take a look at the uploadable résumé on the following page:

Kelly Morgan

100 West Way
city, state, zip
Phone: (987) 654-3210
Email: kmorgan@provider.net

QUALIFICATIONS

Future dietitian with a focus on clinical nutrition, wellness, and sports nutrition

EDUCATION

Master of Science in Nutrition and Food Science
University of Kentucky
Lexington, KY
Graduation Date: May 2017

Bachelor of Science Nutrition and Food Science
Murray State University
Murray, KY
Graduation Date: May 2015
Emphasis in clinical nutrition, wellness, and sports nutrition

WORK EXPERIENCE

Graduate Teaching Assistant
University of Kentucky
Lexington, KY
June 2015 - Present
Assist professor in an Introductory Nutrition course.
Helped develop two new courses on the use of social media for nutritional education and online counseling of patients.
Provide sports nutrition education to student-athletes and coaching staff.

Student Health Liaison
Murray Health Center
Murray, KY
September 2012 - May 2014
Responsible for assisting students with health and wellness inquiries.
Performed diet analysis on student three day food records.
Assisted with various presentations, health fairs, promotions regarding nutrition and health related issues.
Developed handouts, posters and bulletins for promoting health and wellness.
Conducted presentations in student dormitories to promote low-fat living.

HONORS & AWARDS

Outstanding Dietetic Student Award, Academy of Nutrition and Dietetics, 2014
National College Honor Scholarship Society Alpha Chi Member, 2013 - 2014
Scholarship Award, Academy of Nutrition and Dietetics, 2013

MEMBERSHIPS

Academy of Academy of Nutrition and Dietetics, member, 2011 – present
Academy of Academy of Nutrition and Dietetics, Kentucky Student Liaison, 2013-2014
American Culinary Federation, 2010 - present

COMMUNITY SERVICE

Presentation for Northwestern Memorial Hospital Sleep Clinic, 2015
Volunteer, LifeHouse Care Center for Women, 2015
Counselor in the Family Resource Center, Calloway County Schools, 2013-2014
Presentation on allergy awareness to IL HeadStart Organization, 2014

Cover Letters

Another tool you use to get an interview is the **cover letter**. This letter goes with your résumé and tells the reader what job you are applying for and why they should look at your résumé. Your cover letter needs to be direct and to the point, but interesting enough to make the reader take a look at your qualifications. Here's another chance to tell your story, so make it interesting! **If you are sending your résumé attached to an e-mail, the e-mail serves as your cover letter.** If you are uploading your résumé to a website you may also have the option of uploading a cover letter, either as a separate document, or by cutting and pasting it into an online form.

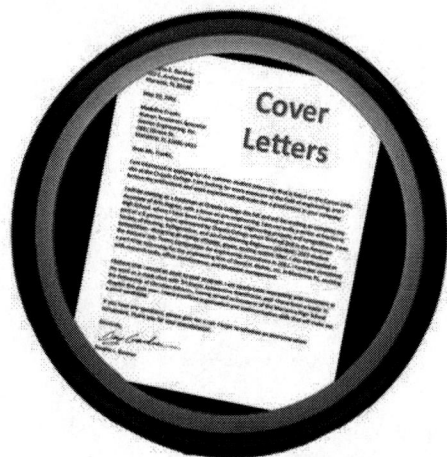

What Goes in a Cover Letter?

Take a look at the cover letter e-mail on the next page for a part time nutritionist position at a gym. Check to see if contains the following details:

- The position you are interested in
- How you heard about the position
- Your qualifications for the position
- A mention of your attached résumé with any links to samples
- Your expectations (getting a call, e-mail, getting an interview...)
- How you can be contacted
- A thank you to the reader.

Dear Ms. Corbett,

Thank you for the opportunity to share my qualifications for the position of part-time nutritionist for the Total Health Workout Center advertised with Indeed.com.

To get right to the point, hire me as an a nutritionist at THWC, and you'll find yourself with a team player and leader in customer education and healthy living with a focus on sports nutrition. You'll have someone with a degree in Nutrition and Dietetics, and the ability to work with all kinds of people, in all states of health and wellness knowledge, skill, and motivation.

As a student health liaison with the Murray State University I worked all aspects of the nutrition training from initial assessment and design to development of customized training to student needs. I believe in spreading the facts about healthy food choices and portion control on my personal blog Power-Food.com. I'm currently pursuing my master's degree in Food and Nutrition, with a specialty in sports medicine, here at the University of Kentucky. I believe in staying on top of new trends and finding new ways to connect with people over wellness topics.

I think my passion for sports nutrition matched with your clientele who are working to make the shift towards a healthy, balanced lifestyle, can be a force for change. I've attached my eRésumé which contains links to some of the marketing pieces I've created, great client comments, and a few links to my blog that focus on targeted eating for cross-training and people with food allergies.

I can be reached most mornings on my cell and after 4:30pm on Tuesdays and Thursdays. I looking forward to the opportunity to connect in person and share more details of what we can create together.

Respectfully,

Kelly Morgan
100 West Way
City, State, Zip
Phone: (987) 654-3210
Email: kmorgan@provider.net

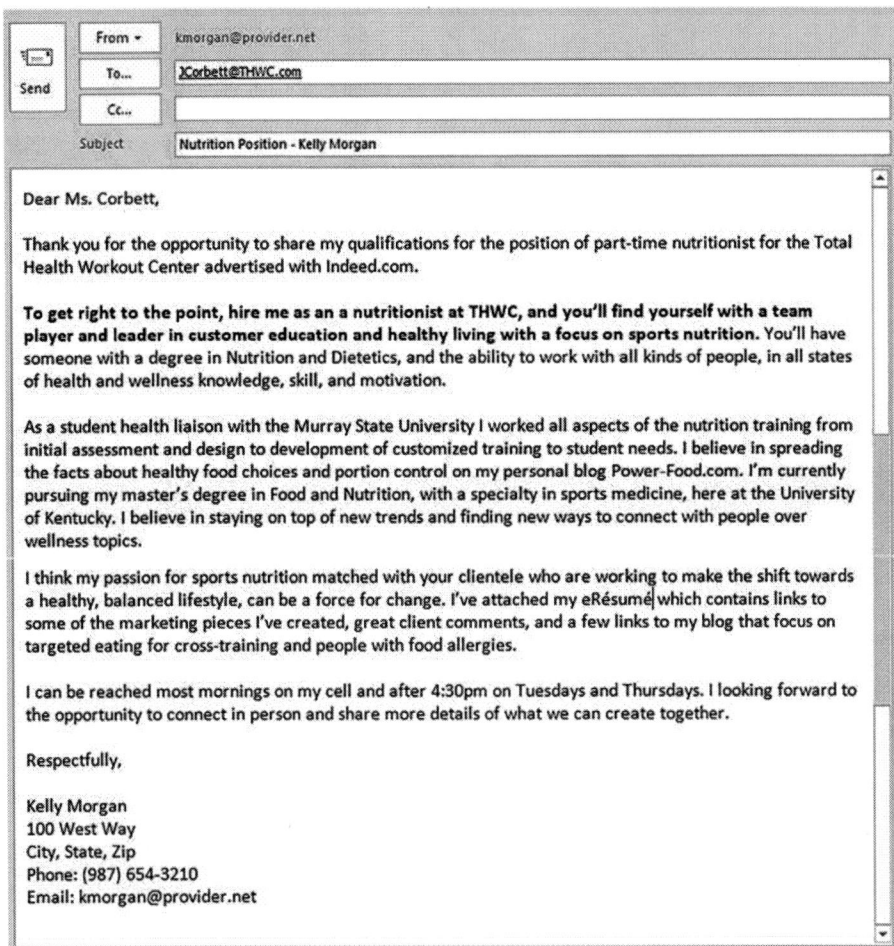

Rules for Writing Good Cover Letters

- **Address the letter to a specific person if possible.**
- **Get to the point!** State your purpose of writing up front in the first sentence.
- **State the action you want to have happen** - Do you want an interview, to receive a phone call, for them to pass your résumé along to others?

- **Be sure to check your spelling and grammar**– Nothing says "I really don't care about this job…" like poor language, spelling errors, and typos.
- **Address any gaps in your cover letter or in the interview, not your résumé**– If you have skill gaps, where you don't have all of the qualifications for the position but you are applying anyway, you will want to emphasize your strengths and your ability to learn new skills in the cover letter.

> **The cover letter is your chance to tell your story, so…**
>
> - **Mention the position you want**
> - **Get to the point**
> - **Tell them the action you want them to take**
> - **Say Thank You**

Types of Cover Letters

There are several different types of cover letters you can create depending on the purpose of your letter.

- **Application letters**– sent when you are applying for a specific position. Be sure to include why you are qualified for the position and why you should be selected for an interview.
- **Inquiry letters**– sent when you know the company is hiring, but they haven't advertised job openings. Inquiry letters should contain information on why the company interests you and why your skills and experience would be an asset to the company. The more you know about the company, the better.
- **Referral letters**– sent when someone you know suggests you contact a particular person in the company. You need to mention the person you know and how they know you. Also mention why that person thinks you would be a good fit for the company.

- **Prospecting letters**– sent to companies to let them know you are interested in jobs that may be currently open or become available in the future.
- **Networking letters**– sent to someone you know to ask for job search advice and assistance. This could include a request for a meeting and letters seeking career advice.

You should shift the content of your cover letter to include the specific information needed depending on the type of letter you are sending.

Your Online Profile and Professional Bio

Just as your résumé gives people an overview of your qualifications for a position, you should create an **online profile** statement for the Internet, giving people a brief overview of who you are and what you have to offer. It usually has a conversational tone, like you're talking to someone face-to-face. This statement could appear on your web page, Facebook™ page or LinkedIn™ profile.

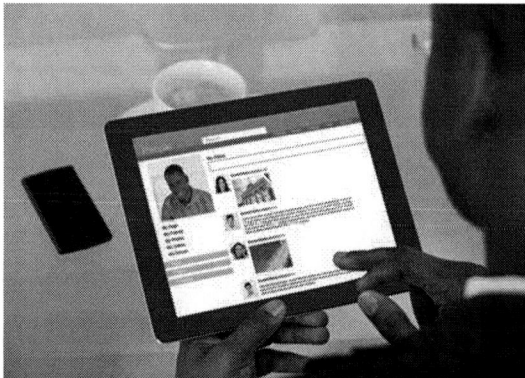

A **professional biography** or "bio" is a more formal version of your online profile and is like a formal introduction. Some people refer to your bio as your "30-second elevator speech." What would you say to someone if you were to give them a 30-second overview of who you are right now? Give your bio to someone when they need to introduce you, or include it with applications for awards and scholarships.

Here's a sample of a dietitian's online profile:

Profile of Kelly Morgan

I'm currently a graduate student and teaching assistant in the Clinical Dietetics program at the University of Kentucky. , and I'm focused on sports nutrition, child obesity, and marketing nutrition to the public. I started out as a dietetic aid which fueled my interest in health and nutrition. I now have a BS in Dietetics and Nutrition from Murray State University. While at MSU I served as a student health liaison, co-chaired a local community outreach program, and authored several articles on healthy living. I share my passion for sharing nutrition food facts and healthy portion control in an online blog- PowerFood.com. I've assisted in the development of two new courses focused on using social media and online nutritional coaching at UK, and expect to become a registered dietitian in 2016. E-mail: kshaw244@gmail.com.

How to Write a Great Profile

- Make it conversational.
- Mention your occupation and accomplishments or your career interest and current status.
- You could also include interests, awards you have received, quotes, beliefs about your chosen profession, professional memberships, community service, and other personal items that make you stand out from the crowd.
- Talk about your skills, your goals, what you have to offer.

Maintain a Good Web Presence

It's a fact that over 80% of employers currently search the Internet to learn about potential employees. That includes social media sites, search engines, forums, gaming sites, etc. It's important to find out how you look online and if needed, clean it up. **Here are a few tips for maintaining a good online presence:**

- **Google™ yourself** and see what comes up.

- **Does your Facebook™ page project you as a good potential employee?** Controversial subjects, questionable photos, and rude language, even spelling and grammar are looked at by recruiters.

- **Set up multiple accounts to keep business and pleasure separate.** Create a LinkedIn™ account to set up a professional profile. Refer business contacts to this site. Use your Facebook™ site for personal use.

- **Use the privacy/profile options to restrict who sees what information on your social media site.** Employers will check out your Facebook™ page and your Twitter™ feeds, so set up separate lists of work and friends, then go to settings/privacy/profile and choose what each group gets to see.

- **Be secure.** Make sure other people don't have access to your accounts.

- **Protect your identity.** Don't reveal key information such as addresses, phone numbers, and full birth dates.

- **Don't post negative info on other people's sites.** If you have done so in the past, see if they can be removed.

- **Keep it clean and think about what you are posting.** Remember, if you put something out there on the web you cannot take it back! If you're in doubt about what's appropriate, ask yourself if you'd like your parents or grandparents to be viewing this information!

- **Keep your work and skill information up-to-date.** Keep a list of places where you post your information and check them to make sure your information is current.

Using LinkedIn™ for Networking

While Facebook™ can be a good tool for connecting to people on a professional level, LinkedIn™ is the online site to use when you want to develop your professional profile. Currently there are about 332 million users on LinkedIn™, and it's becoming the go-to site for employers and recruiters who are getting info on candidates for a position. In 2014, 92% of employers were using LinkedIn™ and 72% were using Facebook™ as part of the hiring process.

With LinkedIn™, you set up an initial profile that includes a professional summary, a list of your experience, education, organizations you belong to, your volunteer experiences and causes, honors, awards, courses you are taking, and projects you've done. In some ways it's like an online résumé. You invite people to link to your page and you receive invitations to link from others. You are building a network of people you know, because you can see not only the people who you know, but the people they are linked to as well. You can also add your key skills to your profile which allows people in your network to give you **endorsements** or recommendations on your skills.

You can use LinkedIn™ to research companies and find people in your network with ties to a specific company or organizations where you want to connect. There are many professional groups and dietetic specialty groups you can join where you can interact and post about topics that interest you. As you participate, people can check out your profile and add you to their network.

Career Smarts

Make sure people can see your career direction in your LinkedIn™ page. Give them a clear vision of your career goals through your headline and summary, the skills and expertise you choose, and the experiences you show. **Your job here is to tease them to connect, not flood them with information. Less is More.**

Here are some of the best tips for using LinkedIn™ in your career:

- **Keep it clean and up-to-date.** Use complete sentences and good grammar. You don't have control about who sees your profile and when, so make sure your updates are complete and you proof what you submit.

- **Upload a professional photo.** Use a head shot with a neutral background. People are 11 times more likely to view your page if you have a photo.

- **Make your profile headline and summary brief and to the point.** You have a few sentences here to really get across who you are and where your focus is in your career. Use those keywords that relate to your skills as you write your summary. This is part of your elevator speech- "tell me about yourself" in the time it takes for a normal elevator ride.

- **Choose the right key skills you want to emphasize.** This should be easy since you are starting to organize your work samples and have chosen focused key skill areas.

- **Use the ACEND® competencies to organize and demonstrate your dietetic skills.**

- **Don't be shy – build your network.** Who should you link to? Invite people you have something in common with, people you know, people who could serve as a reference for you, your teachers, employers, people you met on an internship, neighbors, and even your parents. You never know when a colleague of your mother's just happens to have a connection into the firm you are interviewing with next week.

Writing a Brief Biography

A brief **biography** is a short summary of your qualities and qualifications. Think of it as a short résumé, in paragraph format. A bio is more formal than an online profile, and could be used to introduce you to a group of people when receiving an award, giving a presentation, or working with the media. **Your bio is written in third person, where your online profile is written in first person.** In your career portfolio, the brief bio is placed in front of your résumé. Depending on the situation, you may need a **short bio** or **micro bio** that just gives the basic facts.

When you read someone's résumé you are seeing the facts about a person. **When you read a person's bio, you should feel like you are listening to their story.** It's like a conversation on paper.

Creating Your Biographies

- **For your short bio, start with your online profile.** Rewrite it from first person (I) to third person (he/she.)

Career Smarts

Test out your bio before you need it. There's nothing more embarrassing than standing up in front of a group of people while the moderator rambles on and on from their printed sheet about how wonderful you are- while you stand there trying to look humble.

Take a look at how we rewrote and added details to Kelly Morgan's online profile from earlier in the chapter to create his short bio:

Kelly Morgan is currently a graduate student and teaching assistant in the Clinical Dietetics program at the University of Kentucky where he is focused on sports nutrition, child obesity, and marketing nutrition to the public. Kelly worked for two years as a dietetic aid, which fueled his interest in health and nutrition. He received his BS in Dietetics and Nutrition from Murray State University.

SHORT BIO:
- 1 paragraph containing your most important information
- Use to introduce you to a group or document your credentials.

While at MSU he served as a student health liaison, co-chaired a local community outreach program, and authored several articles on healthy living. He shares his passion for nutrition food facts and healthy portion control in an online blog- PowerFood.com. While at UK, Kelly has assisted in the development of two new courses focused on using social media as an outlet for nutrition information and online nutritional coaching. Kelly plans to become a registered dietitian in 2017. E-mail: kshaw244@gmail.com.

- Cut down the short bio to get the facts for your micro bio.

Kelly Morgan is currently pursuing a graduate degree in Clinical Dietetics at the University of Kentucky. His goal is to take his interests in sports nutrition, child obesity, and nutrition marketing, to impact individuals at a national and local level as a registered dietitian.

MICRO BIO:
- 2-3 sentences with the major facts about who you are
- Use to introduce you to a group or document your credentials.

Every contestant on a game show has a micro bio... in their case, the more interesting and unusual the better!

- Name
- Where they live
- Job
- Interesting fun fact... **that's the** *Jeopardy!™* **bio format.**

Here are some tips to writing a good bio:

- **Include your name in the first sentence** so the reader knows who you're talking about

- **Start with your current occupation and employer.** If you are a student, start with your grade level and school. If you are near graduation, talk about your future plans.

- **If you're using this bio to show your professional accomplishments on the job, look at the key skills and accomplishments you included on your résumé.** If you are a student, look at projects, competitions, and activities that emphasize your expertise in a certain field or area.

- **Put the most important things up front in your bio.** A news reporter always loads the important information at the beginning of a story, knowing that if the article gets cut to fit the space, they can just delete paragraphs from the end of the story. Same goes for your bio.

- **Make it interesting.** Don't give a boring list of everything you can do. How does it sound when you read it out loud?

- **Add more details as needed,** including information on other jobs or interests, awards you have received, quotes, beliefs about your work, inspiring comments, and other personal items that make you stand out from the crowd.
- **Include your e-mail or online media site as a contact** at the end of your bio.

Prep Now!

Keep gathering your work samples. You're now ready to start promoting yourself!

- Create your résumé(s)
  - ▲ Hard copy
  - ▲ eRésumé
  - ▲ Uploadable
- Write a basic cover letter
- Create your online profile
- Set up your LinkedIn™ account and profile
- Write your bios
- Google™ yourself... take a look at how you appear online and clean up your social networking presence if needed.

Step 4: Assembling Your Career Portfolio

At first, your career portfolio may be just a collection of documents, roughly organized by your key skill areas or types of work samples. But eventually, you'll be ready to actually assemble and organize your career portfolio for use in an interview setting or to give people an opportunity to learn about you. In Step 4, you'll learn how to create a hard copy portfolio and look at ways to organize and set up your ePortfolio.

Know Your Target Audience

Your career portfolio should answer the question...

Why Me?

When you're ready to create your career portfolio for show, you've got a purpose in mind. For the most part you want to share your skills and abilities and show why you are the right person. You're in a competition for resources and you need to distinguish yourself from the crowd. Your career portfolio needs to help you answer the key question: Why Me?

You may be interviewing for your first job, competing for an internship or a spot in a specific college program. You might be using it to qualify for a scholarship or document your skills to fulfill the requirements of your degree. You can also use your career portfolio to justify a raise or seek a promotion on the job.

Customize Your Career Portfolio for Every Use

The work samples you show will change based on the reasons behind your career portfolio, whether you are going after a dietetic internship, your first job, or a promotion. Customize your career portfolio each time you use it to target the needs of your viewer. **You have the power to customize and show the samples you believe will connect best for each situation.**

- **What criteria are they using when reviewing your skills and experience?** This will impact the contents you include. What does the reviewer need to see to make good decisions about you?

- **What qualities are they looking for when reviewing you?** What are their expectations? Look at the requirements, whether they are for the job, program, or an application.

Answer these questions, and you have set the guidelines for choosing and organizing work samples with impact.

Contents of a Career Portfolio

The highlight of your career portfolio are your work samples, organized by key skill areas. However, there are other important documents that should also be included in your career portfolio. Here's a list of the basic information you should include, in the order they would appear in a hard copy portfolio:

Items with this icon ⬧ are **tabbed sections** of the career portfolio. Items with this icon ▤ are **pages** in the career portfolio.

Basic Contents of a Career Portfolio

▤ **Statement of Originality & Confidentiality**
(one page that lets people know this is your work and asks them not to copy it.)

▱ **TAB 1: Work Philosophy & Goals**

    ▤ **Work Philosophy** (Your beliefs about yourself, people, and your outlook on work. Use three to five bullet points.)

    ▤ **Goals** (Your career goals for the next two to five years. Use three to five bullet points.)

    ▤ **Professional Bio** (A brief overview of who you are.)

▱ **TAB 2: Résumé**

▱ **TAB 3: Key Skill Area 1:**

    ▤ 3-5 Work samples for your most important skill

▱ **TAB 4: Key Skill Area 2:**

    ▤ 3-5 Work samples for another skill area

▱ **TAB 5: Key Skill Area 3:**

    ▤ 3-5 Work samples for another skill area

▱ **TAB 6: Additional Resources** (includes the following items:)

    ▤ **Faculty & Employer Bio Sheet** (Brief descriptions of the people whose names appear in your career portfolio - who they are and what they do.)

    ▤ **Academic Plan of Study** (A copy of your plan of study listing the courses you have taken to fulfill your degree, if applicable.)

    ▤ **References** (A list of people who can verify your character, academic record, or employment history.)

Remember, this is just a guideline. You can add additional sections as needed for:

- More Key Skill Areas
- Community service
- Internships
- Work in progress.

It's your career portfolio, so if you don't have samples enough for three key skill areas, have two. Don't create an entire section on awards if you've got just one. Look at the skills the sample is showing and include it in one of your key skill areas.

Customize your career portfolio to showcase your best work.

Additional Documents for Your Career Portfolio

There are other documents besides your work samples that go into your career portfolio. These documents are important to help round out and make your career portfolio a complete resource:

- **Statement of Originality** - A basic statement indicating that the career portfolio is your property and should be respected.
- **Summary sheets**– A cover page for each section of the career portfolio including a list of the work samples in that section.
- **Your work philosophy and career goals** from Step 1.
- **Your professional bio or online profile** from Step 2.
- **Academic Plan of Study** - The listing of all the courses required for receiving a degree in your field.
- **Faculty-Employer Bios** - A contact list of people who are mentioned in your career portfolio.
- **References** - List your references and their contact information.

Statement of Originality and Confidentiality

This one-page sheet should be placed at the beginning of your career portfolio. It states that the career portfolio is your work and indicates if certain portions of the career portfolio should not be copied. This can be used as the title page of your career portfolio.

> ## Statement of Originality and Confidentiality
>
> This career portfolio is the work of **Lauren Wilson.** Please do not copy without permission. Some of the exhibits, work samples, and/or service samples are the proprietary property of the organization whose name appears on the document. Each has granted permission for this product to be used as a demonstration of my work.

Template

Download and customize the Statement of Originality. **(stmt of originality** document)

Summary Sheets for Tabbed Sections

Consider creating a **summary sheet** for the beginning of each tabbed section of your career portfolio. This summary sheet lists the samples included in a section of your portfolio, just like a table of contents in a book.

- A summary page can be useful if your career portfolio might be passed around during an interview situation, when you might not be able to explain the contents in person.
- Sometimes seeing the list of samples can cause an interviewer to ask different questions, or find more skills in you than they expect.

Summary Sheet

- **List the dietetic knowledge area and competency area next to each sample.** This shows you understand and meet the competencies that are required to be a dietitian.

- **Consider creating a list of all your samples, organized within each of the five KRD areas and the corresponding competencies.** This can be useful when you want to show you are well rounded and have work samples that demonstrate all the required areas of dietetic knowledge.

- **Consider listing other samples or projects that you didnt include in your career portfolio.** A reader may sometimes see a sample that sparks their curiosity and gets them asking more questions about what you can do.

- **This sheet would need to be customized for any sections that would change as you customize your career portfolio.**

Template

Download and customize the Summary Sheet for your career portfolio. (**summary sheet** document)

Additional Resources in Your Career Portfolio

There are additional documents that should be included in your career portfolio, but are not automatically viewed or looked at during an interview situation. Use ADDITIONAL RESOURCES as the label for the last tab in your career portfolio, and place the following documents behind the tab:

> **Don't forget the Additional Resources section** - it can help your career portfolio stand alone when needed.

- **Faculty/Employer Bios** - A contact list of people who are mentioned in your career portfolio
- **Academic Plan of Study** - A list of the courses you have taken in your academic program
- **References** - A list of your references with contact information.

Faculty and Employer Biographies

The **Faculty/Employer bio sheet** gives basic background information on the people mentioned in your career portfolio. Someone looking at your career portfolio could see who these people are and how they know you. You wouldnt use the bio in the actual interview, but someone viewing your career portfolio by themselves could see the relationships. Put the Faculty and Employer Bio page behind the Additional Resources tab of your career portfolio.

A Faculty/Employer bio sheet should include the following information:

- Name and job title
- Organization
- Areas of specialty
- How you know this person.

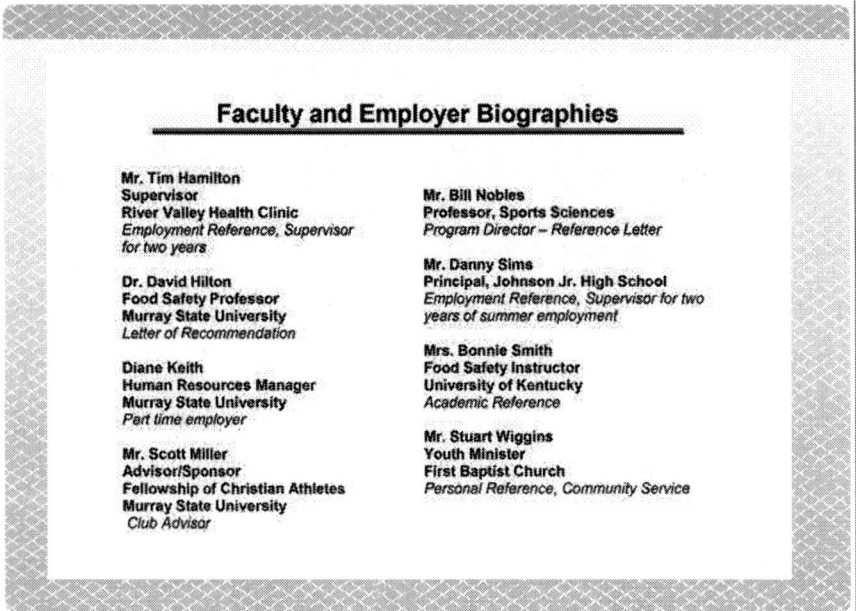

Faculty and Employer Biographies

Mr. Tim Hamilton
Supervisor
River Valley Health Clinic
Employment Reference, Supervisor for two years

Dr. David Hilton
Food Safety Professor
Murray State University
Letter of Recommendation

Diane Keith
Human Resources Manager
Murray State University
Part time employer

Mr. Scott Miller
Advisor/Sponsor
Fellowship of Christian Athletes
Murray State University
Club Advisor

Mr. Bill Nobles
Professor, Sports Sciences
Program Director – Reference Letter

Mr. Danny Sims
Principal, Johnson Jr. High School
Employment Reference, Supervisor for two years of summer employment

Mrs. Bonnie Smith
Food Safety Instructor
University of Kentucky
Academic Reference

Mr. Stuart Wiggins
Youth Minister
First Baptist Church
Personal Reference, Community Service

Template

Download a copy of a faculty and employer bio sheet. (**FacultyEmployer bios** document)

References

Your **references** are a list of people who will speak well about you and your qualifications. Dietetic coordinators expect to see a list of professional references including employers, educators, and people you have worked with on community service projects. For job interviews, companies usually dont worry about your references until they have interviewed you and they are interested in hiring you.

There are three types of references people can give:

- **Employment—** Supervisors, managers, human resource people at your current and previous positions can provide employment references.

- **Academic—** Professors, teachers, counselors, coaches, and people who know your academic abilities can provide academic references

- **Character—** Someone you've worked with in the community, such as church, synagogue or mosque, not-for-profit organizations, clubs, and/or associations can provide good character references.

References

Ms. Fran Adams
General Manager, Heartland Health Services
Bloomington, IL Office: (309) 663-0000
(Internship Preceptor)

Dr. George Wilson
Director of Dietetics, Nutrition, and Sports Medicine
Providence, RI Office: (123) 456-7890
E-mail: gwilson@provider.com
(Academic Reference, Club Adviser)

Robert McCaffrey, RD
Murray State University
Professor
Murray, KY Office: (123) 452-0987

Guidelines for References

- **You should have three to five references an employer can check.** You should include a character, academic, and employment reference.

- **Never use a friend, another employee, or a family member as a reference.**

- **Contact information** - Include the person's name, full title, work address, personal phone, fax, e-mail, and, if given permission, the person's personal phone.

- **For each reference, list the skills, competencies, or achievements the person can address.**

- **Keep these people updated.** You should be certain each of your references has a copy of your résumé and copies of any work samples which refer to them. As long as you keep them as a reference, you should forward them a copy of your résumé each time it is updated, with the changes highlighted.

- **Include a few extra copies of your references in your career portfolio.** If an interviewer asks for a copy of your references, you'll have one to share.

Template

Download a reference sheet template to set up your own reference list. **(References document)**

Academic Plan of Study

Your **academic plan of study** is the list of courses you have taken in school. Classes and requirements vary between schools, and the descriptions of the classes you have taken may help a person decide if you have the background and qualifications needed compared to another person. Look for these descriptions in your course catalog.Highlight any advanced courses or break out and list the description of a class that focused on a specialty area.

- **The academic plan of study is usually placed in the other resources section of your career portfolio** unless you are specifically promoting your education in an area.
- **Get copies of your transcript before you leave school.** If your grades are good, you may want to include a copy of your transcript in the Additional Resources section.

Choosing the Right Work Samples

Take a look at each sample you are thinking about putting in your career portfolio and follow these rules:

- **Keep it relevant**
  - ▲ What skills does this sample show?
  - ▲ Are these skills I want to show?
  - ▲ Does this sample show more than one skill?
  - ▲ Is this showing a technical skill or a soft skill?
- **Make it interesting**
  - ▲ Does this sample keep my interest?
  - ▲ A picture is more interesting than a report
  - ▲ Would I watch this one-minute video clip?
- **Keep it short**
  - ▲ If you have a long report or project, include the table of contents and/or create a summary sheet overview.
  - ▲ Include only part of a large project.
- **Make sure it works**
  - ▲ Is the hyperlink to my video working?
  - ▲ Do you need an Internet connection to view the sample?
  - ▲ Do you need to have a special program or viewer on your computer to play the file?
- **Make sure it looks good**
  - ▲ Are my documents clear or are they blurry?
  - ▲ Are their typos or spelling errors in my letters?
  - ▲ Are recommendation letters printed on company letterhead?

- ▲ Always use copies of certificates, diplomas, cards, awards, etc. Never use the original.
- ▲ Check out the **Style Guide** in the Resource section starting on page 161 for tips on making your documents, photos, and videos look good.

Career Smarts

Each work sample in your career portfolio should serve as a talking point, it should tell a part of your story. What does this sample say about you?

Steps to Assembling Your Hard Copy Career Portfolio

Your hard copy career portfolio is generally used in a face-to-face interview setting. You may be using it to show samples of your work or answer questions asked by the interviewer. It should also be able to stand on its own, because career portfolios often have a pass-around factor. If you have several people involved in an interview, other people may be looking at your career portfolio during the interview, or they may ask to show it to someone else in the department. You want to make sure that every sample is self-explanatory and your career portfolio is easy to navigate.

Assembling Your Hard Copy Career Portfolio

1. Gather your supplies together.

2. Create your tabbed sections and organize your work samples.

3. Develop and print support materials.

4. Assemble and review your career portfolio.

1. Gather your Supplies

- **Zippered 3-ring notebook** - We recommend a zippered binder so nothing falls out and it protects the contents of your career portfolio. Use a high quality binder for a professional look.

- **Sheet protectors**– Each document and work sample should be put into individual sheet protectors so your samples stay neat and have a quality look. Use clear sheet protectors instead of anti-glare for an easier read.

- **Extra-wide 3-ring tabs with labels or stick-on tabs**– Tabs should always extend beyond the sheet protectors and should never be hidden within the samples. You can buy extra-wide tabs that will extend over a sheet protector, or you can buy tabs that stick onto individual sheet protectors.

- **Blank business cards sheets** (Used for sample overview cards)

- **Work samples including your certificates, photos, documents, letters, etc.**

2. Organize Your Tabs and Work Samples

After gathering your work samples and creating your résumé, you should know the key skill areas you want to feature in your career portfolio. It's time to decide which tabs to include in your career portfolio.

We suggest you start with these basic tabs and work from here:

Tab 1: Work Philosophy & Goals.

Tab 2: Résumé.

Tab 3: Key Skill Area 1: (Your title).

Tab 4: Key Skill Area 2: (Your title).

Tab 5: Key Skill Area 3: (Your title).

Tab 6: Community Service.

Tab 7: Additional Resources (last tab).

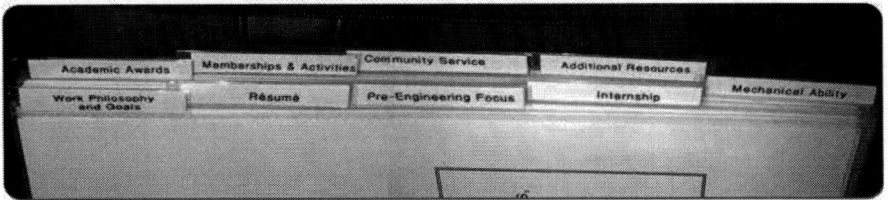

If you have more categories, you can add more tabs as needed to showcase what you can do. Depending on your samples, you might include some of these tabs:

- Activities and Interests
- Memberships
- Awards and Honors
- Internship
- Publications
- International Experience
- Certificates
- Certifications

Here are sample tabs for a dietetic intern:

Tab 1: Work Philosophy & Goals.

Tab 2: Résumé.

Tab 3: Dietetic Internship.

Tab 4: Clinical Experience.

Tab 5: Sports Nutrition.

Tab 6: Training and Education.

Tab 7: Memberships & Activities.

Steps to Assembling Your Hard Copy Career Portfolio

Tab 8: Community Service.

Tab 9: Additional Resources.

A dietitian with a specialty in weight loss and nutrition might have these tabs:

Tab 1: Work Philosophy & Goals.

Tab 2: Résumé.

Tab 3: Clinical Nutrition.

Tab 4: Weight Loss and Training.

Tab 5: Educational Materials

Tab 6: Community Service.

Tab 7: Activities & Interests.

Tab 8: Additional Resources.

If you want to focus on demonstrating the key skill areas needed to be a dietitian, consider using the KRD standards as tabbed areas:

Tab 1: Work Philosophy & Goals

Tab 2: Résumé

Tab 3: KRD 1: Scientific and Evidence Base of Practice

Tab 4: KRD 2: Professional Practice Expectations

Tab 5: KRD 3: Clinical and Customer Services

Tab 6: KRD 4: Practice Management

Tab 7: Food Service

Tab 8: Community Service

Tab 9: Awards & Activities

Tab 10: Additional Resources

The tabs in your career portfolio should reflect your skills and abilities, so feel free to customize.

Use a computer or a label maker instead of printing the labels by hand. Your portfolio will look much neater. You can use extra wide tabs that are sheet protectors, extra-wide paper tabs, or you can attach stick-on tabs to the first sheet protector in each section.

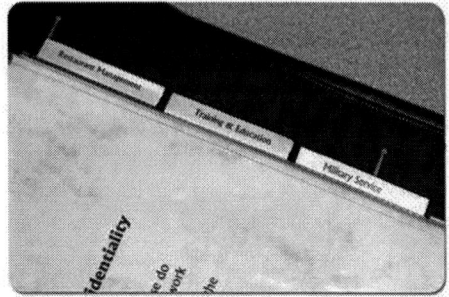

Put each work sample and document page into a sheet protector.

- Use both sides of the sheet protector.
- Each sheet protector should contain two pages of your sample.

If you havent already done so, crea te an overview card or label for each work sample. (Go back to Step 3 for more details on overview cards.) Slide the card inside the sheet protector of the first page of each work sample.

- Work sample overview cards give the basic facts about the sample, letting your career portfolio stand on its own.

Select your best work samples for each section and put them in behind the correct tab. If you have a lot of work samples to choose from, be sure to include only your best samples. Each section should have 3-4 samples.

3. Develop and Print Support Materials

If you haven't already done so, create and print the following items:

- Statement of originality
- Your work philosophy and career goals
- Your professional bio or online profile
- Summary Sheets
- Academic Plan of Study
- Faculty & Employer Bios
- References.

4. Assemble and Review Your Career Portfolio

Now that you've printed any addit ional documents you need, you're ready to do the final assembly. Proofread, review, and test for accuracy and clarity.

Once you have your career portfolio assembled, set it aside for a day and then come back and look at it with fresh eyes.

Here are a few suggestions for review:

- **Read for typos, spelling, grammar, and format.** Proof everything at least three times.
- **Talk through the sections of your career portfolio** as if you are participating in a practice interview.
- **Check to see that your career portfolio reflects your style.**
- **Review your work samples** - If you are unsure about a certain work sample, leave it out.
- **Does your portfolio meet the needs of the interview situation?** Make sure you have selected work samples that will connect with the interviewer and the organization.

Developing Your ePortfolio

There are many different programs you can use to create an ePortfolio. Your school may already have a program in place for you to use. You can also find many commercial programs for purchase that will let you store your work samples, organize them and present them in a specific manner. We cant give the step-by step details to managing your specific ePortfolio program, but there are some basic guidelines to keep in mind when working with ePortfolios.

Assembling Your ePortfolio

1. Learn the capabilities of your software.

2. Upload and organize your samples into key areas.

3. Customize what can be viewed or seen by different people.

Protecting Your Identity

Stop identity theft by protecting your work samples.

- Delete or black out any membership numbers or personal information on certificates or samples.
- Keep personal contact information off work samples that could become public.

Learn the Capabilities of Your Software

Explore your software and find out your options for organizing and sharing the information.

- **Sharing–** What choices do you have when sharing your ePortfolio with others?
    - ▲ Can you set up a special view for specific people?
    - ▲ Can you choose which samples to share for a particular setting?

- How much control do you have over privacy?
- Can you check to see who has viewed your ePortfolio?
- Can you limit the length of time someone has to view your ePortfolio?

- **Organizing**
  - Is it easy for someone else to navigate through the program?
  - What options do you have for organizing samples? Can you assign a keyword or multiple keywords to a sample?
  - Can you choose how samples are grouped? by project, by course, by keyword?

- **Storing Work Samples**
  - Is it easy to upload work samples?
  - Do you have a limit to the number of samples you can load?
  - Can you upload multiple formats such as graphics, audio or video segments?
  - Can you add a label to each sample to describe its purpose and contents?
  - Can you print hard copies of your samples?

Organizing Your ePortfolio

Create your navigation for your ePortfolio to match the key sections of the career portfolio. You may need to explore your software to see if this information is called something different.

- Work Philosophy
- Professional Bio
- Professional Goals
- Résumé
- Work samples by key areas (Give Specific Titles!)
  - 3-4 Key Competency Areas
  - Rare Talent Field

- Community Service (Transferable Skills)
- Professional Memberships
- Degrees, Certifications & Awards
- Plan of Study
- Reference Info
- Load work samples within each appropriate section.

You may need to explore your software and see where this information is stored. Look for places where relevant samples could be uploaded and stored. Your software may not have a section called Work Philosophy, so you might want to upload that as a work sample, or create something under a Goals section of the ePortfolio that would display instead.

General Tips for Working with ePortfolios

- **Choose your best samples.** You may share more samples electronically than in hard copy form. Put your most outstanding work samples first in your presentation.

- **Crosslink work samples where possible** to demonstrate when one work sample can document multiple skills.

  - ▲ You developed a PowerPoint™ presentation on children and food allergies. You could access the sample under **Presentations and Training** (your skill using PowerPoint™) and also under **Clinical Nutrition** (showing your research abilities and content knowledge.)

- **Clearly label each work sample** by targeted skills, competencies and competency areas. A person should know what each work sample shows and the skills it demonstrates.

> **Clearly label your samples so the reader knows exactly what they are viewing**

- **Use icons of samples to speed up load times.** If possible, have your ePortfolio display a small graphic copy of your sample. When clicked, the full-size graphic appears on screen.

- **Use .wav files for voice, etc to show multimedia samples.** Keep samples small, from 30 seconds to 3 minutes maximum.

- **Cross reference to your eRésumé,** including a download of your résumé so individuals viewing the site can follow your choices using the résumé as a map. If you've sent out an eRésumé and are following up with a link to your full ePortfolio, be sure you also include those same samples in your ePortfolio view.

- **Customize your ePortfolio with your work samples to your audience**– See if you can create a different selection of samples for different people. If you have only one link to your samples, consider setting the length of time those samples are available to view. NEVER hesitate to update and refine your site to meet your current needs.

> **If the technology doesn't work, neither do you.**
> **Make sure all your web links work**
> **and your web pages are current.**

Assembling a Career Portfolio for Different Uses

One of the most important things to remember, whether you are assembling your hard copy or ePortfolio, is to customize your career portfolio to each interview and situation. **Your career portfolio is NOT a static document.** You have the power to customize and show the samples you believe will connect best for each situation.

This is very critical if you are competing for a dietetic internship or you are interviewing for several different types of jobs. You want to target the work samples viewed to each specific job. When choosing what to include, keep in mind these factors:

- **Review the purpose of your career portfolio.** Are you applying to an internship, trying to get a new job, or working toward a promotion? The work samples you show will change based on the reasons behind your career portfolio.

- **What criteria are they using when reviewing your skills and experience?** This will impact the contents you include. What do they need to see to make good decisions about you?

- **What qualities are they looking for when reviewing you?** What are their expectations? Review the requirements and expectations for the internship or job application.

> **Know the person who will be looking at your career portfolio.**
>
> Customize your Career Portfolio to his or her needs.
>
> Know the criteria being used to evaluate your skills.
>
> Review the requirements of the internship or job

Answer these questions, and you have set the guidelines for choosing and organizing work samples with impact.

Remember, the biggest value of the career portfolio is in the process of preparing the career portfolio itself. By putting together your career portfolio, you have reviewed your skills and strengths, found samples that prove these skills, and improved your confidence and self-awareness about what you have to offer.

Prep Now

Assembling your hard copy career portfolio

- Gather supplies
- Develop and print support materials including:
  - ▲ Statement of Originality
  - ▲ Summary Sheets
  - ▲ Your work philosophy and career goals from Step 1
  - ▲ Your professional bio or online profile from Step 2
  - ▲ Academic Plan of Study
  - ▲ Faculty & Employer Bios
  - ▲ References
  - ▲ Overview cards for individual work samples
- Assemble your career portfolio for your current use.

Assembling your ePortfolio

- Review the features of your ePortfolio program identifying how to customize and set viewing options
- Check labels on all work samples
- Make sure you select the best work samples for your current needs
- Check links and make sure your navigation is clear and easy to use.

Practice using your career portfolios!

STEP 5: USING YOUR CAREER PORTFOLIO

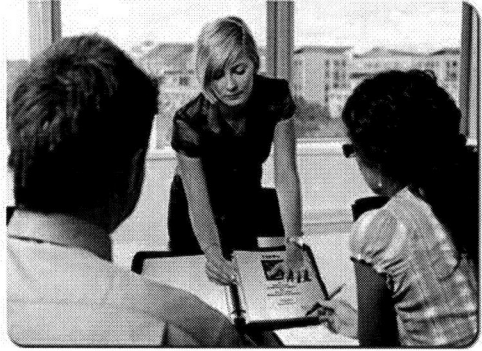

Once you've put together your career portfolio its time to use it! Step 5 is all about how to use your career portfolio to show you are the right person for the position. We build on the assembly step and take it further to how to best use your career portfolio during a face-to-face interview, or as a tool to generate interest and network with other people. One of the greatest strengths of the career portfolio is being able to customize it for different uses. Well take a look at the ways you can use your career portfolio to showcase your strengths, abilities, rare talents, and all the areas that show you are the right person, in the right place, right now.

Your career portfolio grows as your skills grow. With every job you do, every career shift you make, you add to your skills, you switch out old samples for newer, better ones, and you use your career portfolio to document your success on the job and position yourself for advancement.

> **The power of your career portfolio is in your ability to customize it for each use.**

As you assembled your career portfolio in the last step, you organized and chose your work samples to showcase your best work. You also knew who would be seeing it and how they would be viewing your portfolio.

Get Comfortable With Your Career Portfolio

Now that you have your career portfolio together, **practice using it!**

- **Go over each work sample and talk about it like you would in an interview and ask yourself these questions.**
  - ▲ What are the key skills youVe gained with this sample?
  - ▲ What did you learn in this experience?
  - ▲ Why is this a good sample of your work?
  - ▲ Can you tell someone your work philosophy and goals in a conversation without looking at the page?
- **Grab a friend and practice interviewing.**
  - ▲ Have your friend ask you common interview questions, then use your career portfolio to provide the answers.

  - ▲ Dont forget to practice introducing your career portfolio to the interviewer and what it contains.
- **Know the order of your tabs and samples.** You should know your career portfolio backward and forward and be able to read it upside down!

Practicing With Your ePortfolio

When working with your ePortfolio, be sure you:

- **Set permissions correctly** so you control who has access to different areas of your ePortfolio
- **Know how it will display for people who receive the link**
  - ▲ If you are sending a secure link with instructions for accessing your ePortfolio, send it to yourself first and make sure all links and pages come up correctly.
  - ▲ Are all your navigation tags set correctly?

- **Walk through your ePortfolio as if someone else were looking at it**
  - ▲ Does it show the samples you want?
  - ▲ Is it easy to navigate?
  - ▲ Do you have a brief description of each work sample?
- **If you plan to use your ePortfolio during an interview:**
  - ▲ Practice quickly accessing your samples.
  - ▲ Be able to talk about your samples just like it was a hard copy career portfolio.
  - ▲ Make sure you can quickly access the samples you want. Be prepared to show your ePortfolio even when you don't have an Internet connection.

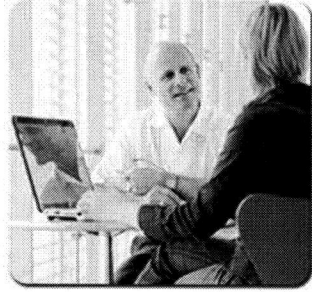

Using Your ePortfolio to Preview Your Skills

Your ePortfolio is one of your best tools to market your skills and introduce yourself to others as you network with people. You identify which skills you want to promote, and then set your ePortfolio to display only certain documents and work samples, then send a link. Here are some of the best ways to use your ePortfolio as a marketing tool:

- **Send a link to your ePortfolio to:**
  - ▲ people on your contact list on LinkedIn™
  - ▲ introduce yourself to possible business connects from friends and family
  - ▲ people you want to use as a business or personal reference
  - ▲ selection committees to provide additional information about you for use in decision making.
  - ▲ a recruiter or interviewer after your job interview as a follow-up.

- ▲ the dietetic coordinator where you would like to have an internship.
- **Add a link to your Facebook™and LinkedIn™pages** - just be careful about who has access to what information.
- **Make sure your ePortfolio and your hard copy portfolio parallel each other.** If you show someone samples from your hard copy portfolio, make sure those same samples are available in any ePortfolio view you send them. You can add more samples to the ePortfolio view, but don't take any away.
- **Limit access to your ePortfolio.** Be sure to decide exactly what someone should be able to see, and use that link. Make sure you keep your ePortfolio up-to-date and verify that the links work correctly. You really need to know the capabilities of your ePortfolio software. You may be able to give someone a link with a limited time-frame for access or secured with a password so your information can only be accessed by specific people you send the link.

Using Your Career Portfolio in a Face-to-Face Interview

Your hard copy career portfolio is the tool of choice when it comes to face-to-face interviews. A hard copy career portfolio is fast and easy to view. You can flip to a page and start talking about your sample without having to scroll a document on a screen or try to zoom in to view a certificate on your tablet. Here are good ways to use your career portfolio in an interview to prove you are qualified for the position- be that a job, internship, scholarship, or raise:

Before the Interview

It's important to be prepared for every interview. You'll feel more confident when you're ready.

Get Your Career Portfolio Ready

- **Be sure you have customized your work samples** to the needs of this particular employer or internship.
- **If possible let the interviewer know you have a career portfolio available,** a hard copy and/or ePortfolio.
- If you've spoken with the interviewer when setting up the interview appointment, **offer to send them a link to your ePortfolio or send an eRésumé with links to your best samples.** This may give your interviewer time to view your samples and have some extra questions ready for your interview.
- **Make sure your career portfolio, résumé, and application all have the same information. Bring these to the interview:**
  - ▲ Your career portfolio
  - ▲ Extra copies of your résumé
  - ▲ A completed job application or internship application (if available)
  - ▲ Note pad and pen.

The Right Way to Act During an Interview:

- ▲ Smile even if you are nervous.
- ▲ Be polite - remember "Please" and "Thank You".
- ▲ Have good eye contact with your interviewer.
- ▲ Have good posture - don't slouch or cross your legs.
- ▲ Turn off your cell phone.

Most interviewers follow a schedule and allow a certain amount of time for the interview, usually 30 to 90 minutes, depending on the level of job. The more experience required, the longer the interview and the more people you may meet. You may be asked to fill out an application before the interview or take an specialized aptitude test for the position. You usually learn about these when setting up the appointment for the interview.

At the beginning of an interview, let the person know that you have your career portfolio available. Watch the interviewer to see if they show any interest.

- If the interviewer is interested and wants to see your career portfolio immediately, you should be able to give a basic overview of your skills and qualifications in 5-8 minutes, unless they ask questions.
- If they arent as interested, thats OK, just refer to your career portfolio when you want to answer any questions.

Physically Showing the Career Portfolio

- **Put the career portfolio facing the interviewer.** Practice ahead of time going through your portfolio upside down, so the interviewer is seeing your portfolio right side up. This is where being able to navigate through your career portfolio inside and out is very helpful.

- **You may want to ask for permission to get up and stand beside the person to talk briefly through the sections.** Follow the lead of the interviewer if they are comfortable with this. Just be sure the interviewer can clearly see the contents of the career portfolio.

- **If you are using a tablet with your ePortfolio, make sure your tablet is easy for them to view.** You may want to use a case with a built-in stand and set it to the side so you can both see the screen.

- **You might also pull up a sample and then hand the tablet to the person to view. Follow their lead.** If they are experienced using a tablet, they will know the basic navigation features of scrolling around the screen or zooming in and out. For the less experienced tablet user, you may need to show the person how they can scroll through the document or zoom in on the details.

Overview Your Career Portfolio

- **If you have an opportunity to present your career portfolio, take 5-8 minutes and:**

  - ▲ **Overview your work philosophy and professional goals-** This shows you have plans and focus. Spend a little time here.

  - ▲ **Point out your résumé and remind the person that he or she already has a copy.** Be sure you have a spare résumé tucked in the inside pocket of your portfolio.

  - ▲ **For each section, describe briefly what the viewer or reader will find.** Let the interviewer decide how much detail to go into in each section.

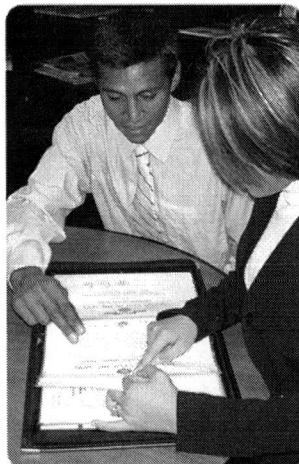

  - ▲ **Dont use the portfolio to shut off questions from the interviewer-** Give enough overview to make the person curious to see more, or ask you additional questions.

  - ▲ **When youre finished showing the po rtfolio, leave it in front of the person.**

- **Keep in mind that your career portfolio is just a tool- not a crutch.** Balance your use of the portfolio during the interview. Remember you are here to talk with the interviewer and answer their questions. If you rely 100% on your portfolio, the interviewer may feel like you need too much help.

- **If you are being interviewed by several people in a group setting, make your portfolio available to all of them.** You may be in a situation where you are talking to one person while another is looking at your career portfolio. Make sure your career portfolio can stand on its own without explanation.

- **Dont be upset if you dont get a chance to use your career portfolio** - There are times when the interviewer has his or her own schedule and you may not be able to use your career portfolio. Dont push your career portfolio on them.follow your instincts.

Using Your Career Portfolio to Answer Questions

Here are some interview questions that could be answered by a look into your career portfolio:

- **"What are your five-year goals?"** or **"What are your future plans?"** (See the work philosophy and professional goals section.)

- **"Why are you a good fit for our program?"** (Focus on the best work samples in your key skill areas and your community service experience.)

- **"How confident are you counseling patients?"** (See the work/ service samples where you interacted with patients, developed brochures and materials, thank you letters from patients you have counseled, a positive review from your coordinator on an internship rotation.)

- **"What do you do for recreation or release?"** (Show them your community service section.)
- **"What was your most difficult class?"** (Show them a work sample from your class.)
- **"Have you ever _____?"** (Fill in the blank and show the person a work or service sample.)
- **What certifications do you hold?** (See the certifications, diplomas, awards, and degrees sections.)
- **"How do you work as part of a team?"** (Show them work samples that you generated as a group project and discuss the group dynamics.)

Remember, the real value of the career portfolio is in the process of preparing the career portfolio itself. By putting together your career portfolio, you have reviewed your skills and strengths, found samples that prove these skills, and improved your confidence and self-awareness about what you have to offer.

Using Your Career Portfolio in a Phone Interview

More companies are using phone and video conferencing meetings to narrow the list of candidates to bring to a face-to-face interview. In most cases you have submitted your application or résumé to a company, and have made the initial cut. This is a good situation where an eRésumé or ePortfolio can be useful.

- **Send the interviewer a copy of your eRésumé once you confirm an appointment.** Sometimes you may get a request for an interview based on a résumé you submitted online, where you haven't included the hyperlinks to your work samples. This gives them time to review your eRésumé or ePortfolio ahead of time and generate questions for you based on your samples.

- **Have a copy of your eRésumé or ePortfolio up on your computer screen while doing the phone interview.** Ideally, your interviewer has it up on their screen too. If so, you can talk the interviewer through your résumé or answer questions by directing them to the appropriate work samples. If they don't have access to the electronic documents during the phone interview, you can pull up your work samples and use it to help you describe your experiences. If you are doing a video conference, you may be able to display your screen to the interviewer, giving you a chance to show some of your relevant work samples.

Be Ready in Advance!

Have your ePortfolio and work samples ready to display before your start the phone interview.

Offer to show relevant work samples when it's appropriate.

- **Send a follow-up e-mail thank you with another copy of your eRésumé or a link to your ePortfolio.** Make a note during the interview of the things that caught the interest of the interviewer and refer back to these in the e-mail. You also might want to modify your eRésumé to include additional samples that might add to your credibility. Never miss an opportunity to make good connections back to the interviewer. Be sure to include all the samples from your hard copy portfolio in your ePortfolio. You can add additional samples as needed, but don't take any out.

Keep in mind that your eRésumé or ePortfolio may be making the rounds of the organization. Interviewers arent the only decision makers in an organization when it comes to hiring. Your eRésumé or ePortfolio will probably be sent on to other people, so make sure you have enough explanation with your work samples to have them stand on their own.

Using Your Career Portfolio As a Follow-up Tool

- **Take time after your interview to debrief -** Were they interested in your career portfolio? Did you feel rushed in presenting it? Did it stay shut in your lap during the whole interview? Think about how you used it and how you can improve. Keep these things in mind for your next interview.

- **Send a thank you letter–** Be sure to follow up with a thank you letter to the interviewer.
  - ▲ Thank you letters should be relatively brief, thanking the interviewer for their time.
  - ▲ Comments about your career portfolio may help jog their memory, and be sure to include the personal comment.
  - ▲ If you didnt get a chance to use your career portfolio in the interview, mention it in your thank you letter. It may create an opportunity for a follow-up interview.
  - ▲ Include a link to your ePortfolio in your thank you letter.

Using Your Career Portfolio in Different Settings

Your career portfolio shifts and changes as your career grows. You may start out using it to **get a summer job** by showcasing your academic record, and community service.

Then, change your career portfolio to help you **compete for your dietetic internship.**

During the internship, you can use your career portfolio to keep **track of all the things you have learned and done on your rotations.** Help your intern coordinator assign you the proper grade and begin to position yourself for the job market.

Then take the best of those samples from your internship and put them into your career portfolio when you are ready to **get a job.** You'll interview better because you can talk about your experiences and show an interviewer what you've accomplished and why you're the right person for the job.

Once you have the job, you can use it to keep track of your accomplishments on the job and be able to show your boss exactly what you do and why you deserve a **raise** or a **promotion.** Use your career portfolio to track the documentation required for your continued professional development and your **PDR (Professional Dietetic Portfolio.)** Many people use a career portfolio to showcase their skills, especially when they are **switching careers**. They want to be able to show how the experiences they have had in the past can apply to a new and different job in another field.

Dietetic Internships

The dietetic internship (DI) is the required practical experience between graduation from a didactic program and professional practice as a registered dietitian. With only 50% of the applicants receiving an internship spot, the whole process is very competitive. Your career portfolio is a tool you can use to help organize your work samples, track your volunteer work experiences, prep your internship applications, and present your qualifications to internship coordinators.

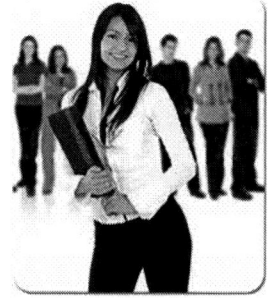

Show How You Fit the Organization

Most people competing for internships apply to three or four programs. Start researching your options ahead of time and look carefully at the description of the program, the various rotations, and requirements for each program. Identify the costs of the program, the number of open slots available, how competitive the internship is, the minimum qualifications, and the flexibility of the program for your needs. Reach out and contact the internship coordinator and talk to them about the opportunity. Go back to Step 1 and review your goals.

- Do you want to complete the internship as soon as possible, or do you want to work on a master's degree at the same time?
- Do you have an area of special interest, and will this internship meet that need?
- Do you have the GPA, job experiences, and volunteer background that will put you at the top of this program's list?

- Does this program meet your needs for location, cost, time, and flexibility?
- What unique skills do you bring to the table?

Use your career portfolio to prepare your applications and show your qualifications.

- Review your career portfolio when writing your personal statements and filling out your applications.
- Identify your skills and rare talents that make you a good candidate.
- Organize your work samples into key skill areas that match the focus and rotations of the internship.
- Showcase your work and volunteer experiences and show how you meet current KRD standards and CRD competencies.
- Offer to send the internship coordinator a link to your ePortfolio.
- Use your hard copy career portfolio in any interview settings.

Career Smarts

Use your Career Portfolio to identify, organize and promote your qualifications for an internship. Before each interview, customize your career portfolio to match the unique requirements and needs of each internship.

Using Your Career Portfolio on Your Internship

You've gotten your dietetic internship and it's your first day on the job. Now it's time to use your career portfolio to document all the skills and achievements you make during your internship.

- **Sit down with your internship coordinator and identify your goals and expectations for the internship.** Look at each rotation you will have, the expectations of the organization and the program.

Identify how you will be evaluated on each rotation. Do you need to document or log your activities? Will you need to write up a summary or complete a weekly checklist?

- **Set up a new tab in your career portfolio for each rotation and capture work samples on the job.** Look at the activities you are doing on the job. Are you generating work samples? Identify the skills you are using and learning on the job. Document any new experiences, tools and technologies you are using in the field and update your career portfolio.

- **Code each work sample with the specific dietetic competencies displayed.** This can be used to prove you are meeting the requirements of the DI.

Confidentiality

Check with your coordinator to make sure you can use samples of company documents or materials in your career portfolio. If you are unsure – ask.

- Be sure not to disclose any confidential information.
- Explain to your supervisor what skills you are trying to document with materials – they may have suggestions for samples you can use in your portfolio.

Keep Updating Your Career Portfolio

- Do a weekly stop and reflect to see what skills you've used or gained this week.

- Create your own skill set document and have your supervisor sign off on your mastery of skills.

- Before the end of your internship, meet with your supervisor to tell them what you've learned and gained from the experience.

- Ask for letters of recommendation or support.

- Update your LinkedIn™ profil e with your new internship information and update your skill list.

- Update your LinkedIn™ Contacts and ask for recommendations of your skills from people you've met on the job.

Use LinkedIn™ to stay connected with the people you meet on your internship.

- Join any LinkedIn™ groups that relate to your specialty area.

- Be sure to take pictures of yourself in action on the job.

- Link to and follow the company.

- Update your résumé and online bio to include your internship.

- Look for mentoring relationships while you are on your internship.

After The Internship

- Update your résumé, and your LinkedIn™ profile.

- Stay active with any professional groups you've joined.

- Document your skills in your career portfolio.

- Ask for letters of recommendation.

- If you are interested in working with them again, keep your connections open.

Using Your Career Portfolio in Different Settings

Using the Career Portfolio for Scholarships and Awards

You can also use your career portfolio to present your qualifications for a scholarship or award. You may be in an interview setting using a hard copy portfolio, or you might need to submit an eRésumé or ePortfolio as proof of your abilities. The type of career portfolio you create should meet the needs of your audience. Here are some guidelines:

> **Your career portfolio shows interviewers that you are an organized person.**
>
> Include your test scores, letters of recommendation, scholarships, awards, activities, etc.

- **Follow Submission Guidelines. Be sure to review the requirements for applying for the specific scholarship or award.** You may be asked to provide specific information and samples in a certain format. If those guidelines are not followed exactly, your application may be rejected out of hand. Be sure that your career portfolio can support the requirements.

- **Determining Your Focus.** What type of scholarship or award are you applying for? This will determine which samples to include and what key skill areas to emphasize. Do you need to prove your connection with a certain ethnic group or interest group? Or, are you going after an scholarship based on your academic record? The samples you use will be very different, and you would place different emphasis on your experience. Be sure to have samples that support this.

- **Customize your eRésumé to meet the need.** Sending an eRésumé may be an appropriate way to present your résumé and qualifications for the scholarship or award. You can customize it to the requirements of the organization and include relevant work samples to show your qualifications.

Using Your Career Portfolio in a Job Search

Your career portfolio should be set up and organized to focus on your qualifications and the skills you have that would make you a good employee for the company.

Employers want to know:

- **Do you have the skills to do the job?**
- **How much training will you need?**
- **Why should I hire you over someone else? Do you have any special or unique skills that will make you a real asset?**
- **Would you be a good fit to the company based on your work ethic, interests, and attitude?**

Does your career portfolio answer these questions?

If you are a student or recent graduate, you are probably applying for entry-level jobs with fewer requirements, and probably a lot of competition. Your career portfolio can help you stand out in an interview as someone who has put some additional effort and thought into the job search. Employers may see that as a good indicator of your ability to work on the job. Remember that your career portfolio is a reflection of who you are, so make it look good!

If you are applying for a job requiring more experience and education, you should know that the hiring process has been changing over the last few years.

- **Hiring an employee can be an expensive process.** It's cheaper to keep an existing employee and promote them instead.
- **Companies are doing more pre-screening** of candidates and actually interviewing fewer people. It's importan t your résumé

and cover letter really promote you as someone who needs to be interviewed.

- **More companies review eRésumés and ePortfolios of candidates** before offering them an in-person or phone interview. More than 80%of companies are using social media to search for candidates.

- **You might have one or two phone or online interviews before you have an in-person interview,** so being able to show your ePortfolio or talk through a sample can be really important.

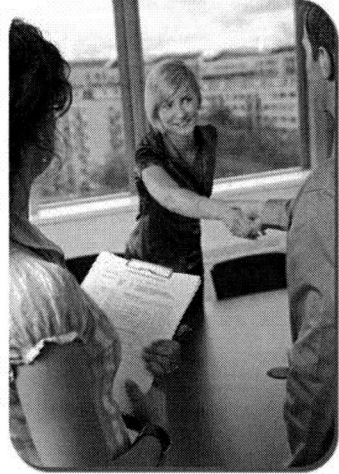

Match Your Skills to the Company

Using a career portfolio for the job search is all about knowing your skills and the skills needed for the job.

- **Review the job posting and job description of the position and match your skill areas to the employer's needs—** What specific skills are required, which are recommended, and which would be nice to have? Make sure your tabbed skill areas match the key skills the employer wants to see.

- **Look at the specific products and services the company provides and match your work samples to their company focus.** If the focus of your job would be in a clinical setting, set up your tabs and use work samples that feature your clinical experiences. If you will have a large component of the job that is patient communication,

create a tab featuring your publications, website, presentations and brochures you've created.

- Show your transferable skills.
- Demonstrate your soft skills that will make you a good employee.
- Show your ability to learn and your willingness to be trained.
- Show your involvement in professional memberships and LinkedIn™groups related to the job.
- Provide any training certifications that qualify you for the job.

Using Your Career Portfolio For Job Reviews

Portfolios are a valuable tool to track accomplishments in your career and your job.

Start collecting work samples from your job that show your skills and abilities. Look at your work assignments, committee work, or service activity, and ask yourself how you would showcase this in your career portfolio.

Track your progress on personal and company goals. If you have specific goals you need to achieve on the job, keep track of them in your career portfolio. Record the dates you were assigned a project and when it was completed. Store work samples showing your accomplishments toward your goals, and you can use these in your next performance review.

Review your job description to identify your skills and competencies. Are there certifications or training that you could request? If you dont have a job description, write one. Look for online resources and samples.

Plan for your performance review. Most job reviews focus on your accomplishments on the job. How well have you done? Are you doing a good job? Are there areas where you need to improve? Think about how you can use your career portfolio to show your boss why you deserve that raise.

- Let your boss know you have a career portfolio several weeks before your review. Most decisions on performance issues and pay raises are made ahead of your review, so give your employer access to your career portfolio before your actual meeting. Your career portfolio should be able to stand on its own without explanation.

> **Tell your boss about your career portfolio a few weeks BEFORE the review.**
>
> **Most performance and pay raises are decided before the actual review meeting.**

Certifications and Your PDP

Use your career portfolio for tracking progress toward certifications and continuing education. The Commission on Dietetic Registration (CDR) requires RDs to attain 75 continuing education credits (CEUs) and DTRs 50 CEUs during a 5-year recertification period. You can find the specific guidelines at www.cdrnet.org. You may choose to take certain classes, attend a workshop, or put in volunteer hours. You can get several different types of certifications:

- **Training or degree program**– once you complete the training program you receive a certification.

- **Course-specific certifications**– you get a certificate once you complete a course or take a test.
- **Regulation-driven certifications**– you are required to take a course or get a certificate.
- **Professional certification**– you must have a certain number of hours of additional training, community service, or other requirements to maintain your credentials.

Use your career portfolio to:

- track participation in professional organizations.
- track requirements completed toward certification.
- present your qualifications and finished materials in a professional way.
- organize your CPEUs in case you need to show documentation of your achievements in a random audit.

Using Your Career Portfolio to Get A Promotion

A promotion interview is basically a job interview for an internal position. Look at the job description for the new position and make sure your work samples show why you are qualified for the job. Show the things you've done in yo ur current position that will help you excel in the new job.

You should already know the players who will be involved, and what they are looking for. They also know something about you and how you currently impact the company. With performance reviews and promotions, most decisions are made prior to the actual review, so you want to get your career portfolio in their hands before the interview itself.

Before the Interview

Notify your supervisor or reviewer of the fact that you have available a career portfolio prepared for this review. Give your supervisor time to review your career portfolio before the decisions have been made. This may be one to two weeks before your review meeting. You have organized the career portfolio to meet the needs of the review as suggested in Step 5.

- Make sure all individuals involved in the promotion interview have access to your career portfolio.
- Send a letter ahead of your interview notifying them that you have the career portfolio available for review.
- Send the link to your ePortfolio so they can look at it ahead of time. It's important your career portfolio can stand on its own with adequate explanation.
- Make sure you have the actual career portfolio with you during the interview.
- Your career portfolio may be passed around to other management individuals. You may have the opportunity to get mentoring advice from others.

Keeping Your Career Portfolio Current

Your career portfolio is a living document, a reflection of who you are and what you can do. You never stop growing and changing, and neither should your career portfolio! (OK, your career portfolio can get too big, but when it does, you'll switch out and refresh your work samples or add additional tabs for new skill areas, etc.)

Career Smarts

Promote yourself within your organization by talking with your supervisor about taking on additional responsibilities and training. Volunteer for special projects and events, let those around you know your career aspirations and how these goals match the organization's needs.

You've worked hard to create your career portfolio, so be sure to take the time to keep it updated.

- **Once a month, make a list of what you have accomplished, planned, and have in progress.** Send yourself a reminder to schedule the time, and dont put it off!

- **Take time at the beginning of each quarter or semester to update your career portfolio.**
  - ▲ Review your work and any classes from the previous semester, saving any projects or work samples.
  - ▲ Create work sample overview cards for your projects and put pages into sheet protectors.
  - ▲ Take photos of any projects too big to fit in your career portfolio.
  - ▲ Request any letters of recommendation from your teachers.
  - ▲ Take a look at your course descriptions from the new semester. Use the Course Tracking template to keep track of your skills and accomplishments.

- **Keep your filing system up-to-date and make frequent backups.** Save copies of each project, report, or other documentation.

- **As you are updating your career portfolio, remember to update your résumé at the same time.** By routinely updating these materials, maintaining your career portfolio will be effortless. Use whatever tools you have available such as electronic calendars, cell phones, or other devices to send you a reminder that it is time to update.

Set your online calendar or cell phone appointment reminder to review and update your career portfolio materials. If you set aside a certain amount of time each month, this review will become a good habit.

Keeping Your Career Portfolio Current

As you work with your career portfolio on a regular basis youll come to appreciate how much your career portfolio lets you show off your skills and abilities to the best of your advantage. Remember, your career portfolio is a tool for life- your life and your career. Success!

Prep Now

- Customize your career portfolio for your current need.
- Know your career portfolio inside and out before your interview.
- Practice, Practice, Practice! Work with a friend to do mock interviews, planning for questions, and practice using your career portfolio.
- Review your career portfolio and performance after each interview. Identify samples that worked well, items that were missing, and any changes you would make to your career portfolio.
- Develop a plan for keeping your career portfolio up-to-date .Customize your career portfolio for each need.

RESOURCE GUIDE

This resource guide contains the following materials designed to help make the development of your career portfolio easier:

1. **Supply List** - Materials to purchase.

2. **Emergency Instructions for Career Portfolio Assembly** - When you need to put together a career portfolio fast...

3. **Action Verbs** - A list of verbs used when describing what you have done. Typically used on your résumé and in goal setting.

4. **Action Verbs by Skills in Industry** - A higher level list of action verbs used by professionals in different industries.

5. **Department of Labor SCANS** - A listing of general skills and competencies. Useful when setting up skill sets and looking up résumé language.

6. **Transferable Skills** - A listing of skills you can use in many different jobs and situations.

7. **Downloadable Templates** - A listing of the files and templates that can be downloaded from the Internet.

8. **Style Guide** - Guidelines for formatting and working with text, graphics, and video files.

9. **Common Job Titles and Skills in Dietetics /Model Job Descriptions** - Samples of dietetic related job descriptions with breakout of KSAs, job tasks, education requirements, tools and technology, etc.

10. **Dietetic Work Samples** - Types of work samples to collect for your Career Portfolio.

11. **Common Dietetics Professional Abbreviations.**

12. **ACEND® Knowledge and Competency Standards**

1. Supply List

Take this list with you to the office supply store. You can also find these items on the Internet at **http://www.officedepot.com** or **http://www.staples.com**

- **Plastic file tote box** (1)
- **Hanging file folders, standard file size** (20–30)
- **Zippered 3-ring notebook** (preferably leather or simulated leather)
- **Clear sheet protectors** (50–100) Different weights are available
- **Extra-wide 3-ring tabs with labels** (1–2 sets)
  There are two different types of tabs available: Tabbed sheet protectors and extra-wide paper tabs.
- **Stick on labels**- an option to the extra-wide 3-ring tabs
- **Blank sheets of business cards** (10 sheets)
- **8-1/2 x 11 plastic photo sheet holders** (2–3 as needed)
- **Nameplate or vinyl self-adhesive business card pocket** for the front cover
- **Paper (high quality).**
  For inkjet printing: use 24# bright white paper

2. Emergency Portfolio Instructions

I Need a Portfolio Now!!!

"Oh, it won't take that long to put it together."

"I have one that I used last time."

"They asked me to bring samples of my work, and the interview's tomorrow!"

"My interview is tomorrow and I have to do all this before I can start on my career portfolio?"

"Do I update my career portfolio, or do I sleep and shower?"

If you've just purchased this book and want to put together a hard copy career portfolio for an interview tomorrow morning, or if you've had this book for a while and suddenly your interview is upon you, there's still hope. Based on several frantic experiences of our own, rest assured you can put together a basic hard copy career portfolio in three hours if you have a computer, printer, and your best friend's help.

Run to the Office Supply Store and Buy...

- Zippered 3-ring binder
- Clear page protectors (a box or two of 50)
- Extra-wide page tabs
- High quality paper
- Extra ink cartridges (if you're using an inkjet printer).

Grab Your Best Friend and...

- Your box of work samples or file of projects
- A computer and printer
- Your most recent résumé.

We can't stress enough the importance of having a friend help you with the assembly process. Friends can help you make wise choices for work samples, determine your management philosophy and goals, stuff paper into page protectors, make up tabs and exhibit cards, and help you through this somewhat frantic time. A good friend serves as a sounding board and tends to ask questions of you that you wouldn't think of yourself.

Include These Sections in Your Portfolio

- Work Philosophy
- Career Goals
- Résumé
- Skill Areas— Determine different areas. Use the KRD standards as tabbed areas if you want to focus on how you meet those competencies. Place work samples behind the appropriate tabs.
- Community Service— Include any work samples and letters available
- Letters of Recommendation (if available)
- List of Professional Membership and Awards
- References.

Don't Forget to...

- Create tabs for each section
- Make up overview cards for your work samples on plain paper.

Review Step 4 on Assembly for specific guidelines for each of these sections.

3. Action Verbs

Action verbs are used in your résumé to indicate the types of actions you have done. Action verbs can be used in present tense to indicate things you are currently doing.

Accomplished	Equipped	Organized
Achieved	Established	Paid
Adapted	Evaluated	Performed
Adjusted	Expanded	Persuaded
Administered	Expedited	Planned
Advanced	Filed	Presented
Analyzed	Furthered	Processed
Assessed	Gained	Produced
Assisted	Generated	Programmed
Authorized	Guided	Provided
Budgeted	Handled	Recommended
Built	Helped	Reduced
Chaired	Implemented	Repaired
Combined	Improved	Reported
Communicated	Increased	Researched
Completed	Initiated	Reviewed
Composed	Instructed	Revised
Conducted	Interviewed	Screened
Coordinated	Introduced	Served
Created	Learned	Set up
Delegated	Led	Simplified
Designed	Located	Strengthened
Developed	Maintained	Supervised
Directed	Managed	Supported
Displayed	Maximized	Taught
Edited	Modified	Trained
Employed	Motivated	Typed
Encouraged	Negotiated	Updated
Enhanced	Operated	Wrote
Enlarged	Ordered	

4. Action Verbs by Skills in Industry

General Achievements

Accelerated	Discovered	Expedited	Mastered	Reduced
Achieved	Doubled	Founded	Originated	Spearheaded
Attained	Earned	Improved	Overcame	Strengthened
Completed	Eliminated	Increased	Overhauled	Transformed
Convinced	Expanded	Launched	Pioneered	Upgraded
				Won

Management Skills

Administered	Coordinated	Handled	Organized	Revitalized
Analyzed	Decided	Implemented	Oversaw	Scheduled
Assigned	Delegated	Improved	Planned	Spearheaded
Attained	Developed	Increased	Prioritized	Strengthened
Chaired	Directed	Inspired	Produced	Supervised
Conceived	Encouraged	Led	Recommended	Transformed
Consolidated	Evaluated	Managed	Reorganized	
Contracted	Executed	Motivated	Reviewed	

Communication Skills

Addressed	Defined	Interpreted	Promoted	Summarized
Arbitrated	Developed	Lectured	Proposed	Translated
Arranged	Directed	Mediated	Publicized	Wrote
Authored	Drafted	Moderated	Published	
Co-Authored	Edited	Motivated	Reconciled	
Collaborated	Enlisted	Negotiated	Recruited	
Corresponded	Formulated	Persuaded	Resolved	
Counseled	Influenced	Presented	Spoke	

Technical Skills

Clarified	Diagnosed	Inspected	Published	Summarized
Collected	Evaluated	Interpreted	Reported	Surveyed
Compiled	Examined	Interviewed	Researched	Systematized
Critiqued	Extracted	Investigated	Reviewed	
Detected	Identified	Organized	Studied	

Research Skills

Analyzed	Designed	Maintained	Remodeled	Upgraded
Assembled	Devised	Operated	Repaired	
Built	Engineered	Overhauled	Solved	
Calculated	Fabricated	Pinpointed	Trained	
Computed	Installed	Programmed	Troubleshot	

Medical Skills

Aided	Diagnosed	Identified	Served
Assisted	Evaluated	Increased	Strengthened
Consulted	Examined	Performed	Studied
Decreased	Handled	Rehabilitated	Trained
Detected	Helped	Researched	Treated

(continued)

Creative Skills

Acted	Developed	Innovated	Pioneered	Streamlined
Composed	Directed	Instituted	Planned	Structured
Conceived	Discovered	Integrated	Produced	
Conceptualized	Established	Introduced	Revised	
Created	Fashioned	Invented	Revitalized	
Customized	Founded	Originated	Set Up	
Designed	Illustrated	Performed	Shaped	

Teaching Skills

Adapted	Coordinated	Explained	Lectured	Team-Taught
Advised	Defined	Facilitated	Persuaded	Trained
Clarified	Developed	Guided	Presented	Tutored
Coached	Enabled	Informed	Set Goals	Updated
Communicated	Encouraged	Initiated	Stimulated	
Conducted	Evaluated	Instructed	Taught	

Clerical Skills

Approved	Compiled	Implemented	Prepared	Specified
Arranged	Dispatched	Inspected	Processed	Systematized
Assembled	Edited	Listed	Purchased	Tabulated
Catalogued	Executed	Monitored	Recorded	Validated
Classified	Filed	Operated	Retrieved	
Collected	Generated	Organized	Screened	

Financial Skills

Adjusted	Audited	Computed	Managed	Reduced
Administered	Balanced	Developed	Marketed	Researched
Allocated	Budgeted	Estimated	Planned	Sold
Analyzed	Calculated	Forecasted	Projected	
Appraised	Compared	Increased	Reconciled	

Helping Skills

Aided	Demonstrated	Gave	Referred	Supported
Assessed	Diagnosed	Guided	Rehabilitated	Taught
Assisted	Educated	Helped	Reinforced	Trained
Clarified	Encouraged	Inspired	Represented	Verified
Coached	Expedited	Motivated	Resolved	
Consulted	Facilitated	Participated	Served	
Counseled	Familiarized	Provided	Strengthened	

Sales Skills

Built	Distributed	Increased	Ordered	Supervised
Collected	Doubled	Installed	Performed	Tripled
Conducted	Expanded	Launched	Performed	
Convinced	Expedited	Managed	Sold	
Delivered	Improved	Negotiated	Streamlined	

5. Department of Labor SCANs

Here is a list of baseline skills and competencies established by the Department of Labor, known as SCANS. Use this skill list to review and organize your own skill sets or to assist in writing your skill descriptions for your résumé.

The Foundation— Competency Requirements:

Basic Skills

- Reading
- Writing
- Arithmetic
- Mathematics
- Speaking
- Listening

Thinking Skills

- Thinking creatively
- Making decisions
- Solving problems
- Seeing things in the mind's eye
- Knowing how to learn
- Reasoning

Personal Qualities

- Individual Responsibility
- Self-esteem
- Sociability
- Self-management
- Integrity

Competencies—Effective Workers can Productively Use:

Resources

Allocating:
- Time
- Money
- Materials
- Space
- Staff

Interpersonal Skills

- Working on teams
- Teaching others
- Serving customers
- Leading
- Negotiating
- Working well with people from culturally diverse backgrounds

Information

- Acquiring and evaluating data
- Organizing and maintaining files
- Interpreting and communicating
- Using computers to process information

Systems

- Understanding social, organizational, and technological systems
- Monitoring and correcting performance
- Designing or improving systems

Technology

- Selecting equipment and tools
- Applying technology to specific tasks
- Maintaining and troubleshooting technologies

From SCANS—Secretaries' Commission on Achieving Necessary Skills. 2011, U.S. Department of Labor

6. Transferable Skill List

Verbal Communication

- Perform and entertain before groups
- Speak well in public appearances
- Confront and express opinions without offending
- Interview people to obtain information
- Handle complaints in person and over the phone
- Present ideas effectively in speeches or lecture
- Persuade/influence others to a certain point of view
- Sell ideas, products, or services
- Debate ideas with others
- Participate in group discussions and teams.

Nonverbal Communication

- Listen carefully and attentively
- Convey a positive self-image
- Use body language that makes others comfortable
- Develop rapport easily with groups of people
- Establish culture to support learning
- Express feelings through body language
- Promote concepts through a variety of media
- Believe in self-worth
- Respond to nonverbal cues
- Model behavior or concepts for others.

Written Communication

- Write technical language, reports, manuals
- Write poetry, fiction, plays
- Write grant proposals
- Prepare and write logically written reports
- Write copy for sales and advertising
- Edit and proofread written material
- Prepare revisions of written material
- Utilize all forms of technology for writing
- Write case studies and treatment plans
- Demonstrate expertise in grammar and style.

Train/Consult

- Teach, advise, coach, empower
- Conduct needs assessments
- Use a variety of media for presentation
- Develop educational curriculum and materials
- Create and administer evaluation plan
- Facilitate a group
- Explain difficult ideas, complex topics
- Assess learning styles.

(continued)

Plan and Organize

- Identify and organize tasks or information
- Coordinate people, activities, and details
- Develop a plan and set objectives
- Set up and keep time schedules
- Anticipate problems and respond with solutions
- Develop realistic goals and action to attain them
- Arrange correct sequence of information and actions
- Create guidelines for implementing an action
- Create efficient systems
- Follow through, ensure completion of a task.

Counsel and Serve

- Counsel, advise, consult, guide others
- Care for and serve people, rehabilitate, heal
- Demonstrate empathy, sensitivity, and patience
- Help people make their own decisions
- Help others improve health and welfare
- Listen empathically and with objectivity
- Coach, guide, encourage individuals to achieve goals
- Mediate peace between conflicting parties
- Knowledge of self-help theories and programs
- Facilitate self-awareness in others.

Create and Innovate

- Visualize concepts and results
- Intuit strategies and solutions
- Execute color, shape, and form
- Brainstorm and make use of group synergy
- Communicate with metaphors
- Invent products through experimentation
- Express ideas through art form
- Remember faces, accurate spatial memory
- Create images through sketches, sculpture, etc.
- Utilize computer software for artistic creations.

Interpersonal Relations

- Convey a sense of humor
- Anticipate people's needs and reactions
- Express feelings appropriately
- Process human interactions, understand others
- Encourage, empower, advocate for people
- Create positive, hospitable environment
- Adjust plans for the unexpected
- Facilitate conflict management
- Communicate well with diverse groups
- Listen carefully to communication.

(continued)

Leadership

- Envision the future and lead change
- Establish policy
- Set goals and determine courses of action
- Motivate/inspire others to achieve common goals
- Create innovative solutions to complex problems
- Communicate well with all levels of the organization
- Develop and mentor talent
- Negotiate terms and conditions
- Take risks, make hard decisions, be decisive
- Encourage the use of technology at all levels.

Management

- Manage personnel, projects, and time
- Foster a sense of ownership in employees
- Delegate responsibility and review performance
- Increase productivity and efficiency to achieve goals
- Develop and facilitate work teams
- Provide training for development of staff
- Adjust plans/procedures for the unexpected
- Facilitate conflict management
- Communicate well with diverse groups
- Utilize technology to facilitate management.

Financial

- Calculate, perform mathematical computations
- Work with precision with numerical data
- Keep accurate and complete financial records
- Perform accounting functions and procedures
- Compile data and apply statistical analysis
- Create computer-generated charts for presentation
- Use computer software for records and analysis
- Forecast, estimate expenses and income
- Appraise and analyze costs
- Create and justify organization's budget to others.

Administrative

- Communicate well with key people in organization
- Identify and purchase necessary resource materials
- Utilize computer software and equipment
- Organize, improve, adapt office systems
- Track progress of projects and troubleshoot
- Achieve goals within budget and time schedule
- Assign tasks and sets standards for support staff
- Hire and supervise temporary personnel as needed
- Demonstrate flexibility in crises
- Oversee communication, e-mail.

(continued)

Analyze

- Study data or behavior for meaning and solutions
- Analyze quantitative, physical, and/or scientific data
- Write analysis of study and research
- Compare and evaluate information
- Systematize information and results
- Apply curiosity
- Investigate clues
- Formulate insightful and relevant questions.

Research

- Identify appropriate information sources
- Search written, oral, and technological information
- Interview primary sources
- Hypothesize and test for results
- Compile numerical and statistical data
- Classify and sort information into categories
- Gather information from a number of sources
- Patiently search for hard-to-find information
- Utilize electronic search methods.

Construct and Operate

- Assemble and install technical equipment
- Build a structure, follow proper sequence
- Understand blueprints and architectural specs
- Repair machines
- Analyze and correct plumbing or electrical problems
- Use tools and machines
- Master athletic skills
- Landscape and farm
- Drive and operate vehicles
- Use scientific or medical equipment.

from Life Work Transitions.com

©1999–2011 by Deborah L. Knox and Sandra S. Butzel, Butterworth-Heinemann

7. List of Downloadable Templates

You can download template files to help you save time while creating your career portfolio.

Download the template files at:
http://www.learnovation.com/d2-templates/

or scan the QR code at the right with your phone to go directly to the web site.

Use these documents as a starting point. Customize these files and make them work for you. Feel free to change the fonts and rearrange information as needed.

Academic Planning Tool– A four-year course planner for tracking classes towards a degree.

Career Planning Tool– A form to help you identify key skill areas and work samples in your career portfolio and eRésumé.

Course Tracking Tool– A form to help track skills and work samples from classes.

Faculty Employer Bios– A contact list of people who are mentioned in your career portfolio.

Overview cards– Business card layout for printing overview cards used to identify work samples and materials in your career portfolio.

Recommendation request– A sample letter for requesting a recommendation letter.

References– List your references and their contact information.

Skill Set– A blank skill set serves as a starting point for creating checklists of your skills.

Statement of Originality– A basic statement indicating the career portfolio is your property and should be respected.

Summary Sheet– A one-page overview of a tabbed section of the career portfolio, listing samples included in the section.

Work Philosophy & Goals– List your work philosophy and career goals.

8. A Matter of Style

You need to make sure your career portfolio has a professional appearance. If your portfolio looks sloppy and disorganized, don't even bother to take it to the interview or meeting. Your portfolio must look as clean, organized, and professional as you do.

The focus of this section is on style: the look, feel, and presentation of the materials in the portfolio. **This section provides some basic guidelines for producing your work samples and other documents in your portfolio by taking a look at:**

- **working with words and pictures** (text and graphics).
- **production tips for video and photography.**
- **physical production of materials** using copiers, scanners, and printers.

Text

Just as important as the words you use is the look and feel of the text. The following section will give you ideas for improving the style of your words.

- **Proof your work—** Proofing your work ensures a professional look and feel to the documents you produce. Spelling, punctuation, or grammar errors can be embarrassing.
- **Use bullet points—** Bullets are an easy way to organize information in a readable, concise way. You've probably noticed after reading through this book that we, the authors, love to use bullet points. Here's a bulleted list of some of the reasons to use bullet points:
- Bullets are used to:
  - highlight key points in the text.
  - make it easier to quickly scan through information.

- ⏶ list several points or examples.
- ⏶ eliminate unnecessary text from sentences.

Now, take a look at the same information, written in paragraph form rather than using bullets and decide which is easier to read:

Bullets pull out key information and make it easier for a reader to quickly scan through a lot of information. Bullets are often used when you are listing several points or examples. They also can eliminate unnecessary text from sentences.

Fonts

The look and style of the letters in your documents come from the fonts. Fonts are one of the simplest ways to control the look of your document and can be used to let your creativity and personality flow onto the page.

Serif vs. sans serif fonts— There are thousands of fonts available these days. All of these fonts fall into two major categories: serif or sans serif. Each of these groups has a different look and can be used to emphasize specific pieces of information in the document.

Serif fonts have the little flourishes at the ends of letters. Notice the curve of an "a" or the edges on a "T" below.

Examples of serif fonts are:

Times New Roman   Garamond   Bookman Old Style

Sans serif fonts don't have the flourishes and curves in the letters. The font you are reading now is a sans serif font called Franklin Gothic Book.

Examples of sans serif fonts are:

Arial   Humanist   Dom Casual   Tahoma

Decorative fonts— Be careful when you use decorative and funky fonts. These can be serif or sans serif. They are great for projects and section pages in your portfolio, but don't use them as main text in a document. They are hard to read. Use them as accent only, and never on a résumé. Examples of decorative fonts include:

Marydale   *Party*   **Burweed ICG**   Treefrog

Guidelines for Font Usage

There are no strict rules for the use of fonts, but here are some general guidelines:

- **Use serif fonts for body text**— Serif fonts are easier to read because our eyes use the little flourishes on letters to distinguish the letters. Most of the books you read are in a serif typestyle.

- **Use sans serif fonts for headings**— Sans serif fonts are often used for headings and titles rather than text. They are used to capture interest and draw attention to a particular section.

- **Bold and *italic*—** The same goes for bold and *italic*: use them sparingly, when you need something emphasized.

- **Avoid underlining text!**— <u>Underlining is a tool that was used in the era of the typewriter, when we didn't have bold and italic.</u> Don't use it.

- **Leave only one space after a period**— There was an old typing rule about leaving two spaces after a period so you could easily see the end of a sentence in the typewriter age. With the advent of word processors and proportional fonts, we don't need the extra space.

- **Choose the correct font sizes**— The size of the font also affects the readability of the document. The most common size is 12-point. This book is written in 12-point font to make it easy to read at a glance. Ten point is the smallest size we recommend using on résumés and other documents. Any smaller, and it is very hard to read. The text in footers and headers can be smaller than 10-point, as long as they are still readable.

- **Use spell check—** All good word processors contain a program to check spelling. Use this to correct typing and spelling mistakes. OK, this is an obvious step, but it's amazing how many documents we see where this simple, convenient step was overlooked. Typos look bad (especially on the front page of your portfolio!)

- **Don't rely on the spell checker—** Proof your work. Too many people rely on the spell checker to catch all their mistakes. Unfortunately the spell checker can't recognize words that are spelled correctly but misused in a sentence.

  - ▲ (You no that I'm talking about, don't ewe?— You know what I'm talking about, don't you?)

Margins, Tabs, and Spacing

The margins, tabs, and spacing you use in a document will change depending on what you are producing. Keep in mind how the document will be used when setting up the page.

Here are some general rules:

- **Single space your text—** You're probably familiar with single and double spacing. Double spacing is commonly used for reports, but single spacing should be used for most of the documents in your portfolio. Generally, you leave a double space between headings and the body of the text.

- **Use a generous margin around the page—** Allow a generous margin around your page, generally 3/4 to 1" around the entire page. Don't make your margins any smaller than 1/2", or your page will look crowded. Many people like to make notes in the margins of a résumé during an interview, and good use of white space in the form of margins allows this. Wider margins also give documents a clean and open look.

- **Don't be afraid to go to a second page—** Two or three balanced, open pages look much better than one cramped page. Keep in mind the information in your documents should be important. Don't go to two pages when you can trim out unnecessary details.

- **Keep the style consistent**— Decide on a look and style for your portfolio documents and then stick with it. Use the same margins, fonts, and spacing on these documents.

Visual Media—Working with Pictures and Video

A picture is worth a thousand words. It is very important to get your pictures to look their best in order to convey the right impression. There's no question that we learn more quickly from pictures than from words on a page. Like anything else in your portfolio, pictures and videos should demonstrate your ability to perform a specific skill or competency and should be used when words won't convey this or would take too long.

Photographs

Photographs are used to emphasize your work. Take the best shots that demonstrate your work, but don't include too many photos. Photographs can be useful when you want to:

- **Display a finished product**— Displays, posters, special campaign materials, booths you have created for a health fair, etc.

- **Put your talents on display**— Public speaking, training sessions, meetings, television appearances, anywhere you are in action.

Tips for Taking Better Photographs

- **You should appear in the photo when possible**— This provides proof that it's your work, not someone else's.

- **If you're working with a digital camera**— Shoot your photos at the highest quality setting. The higher the quality (resolution) of the picture, the better your print will be. You will also be able to blow up or reduce the photo and still have a good quality picture.

- **Get close**— Get close to your subject (unless you're photographing wild animals!). Use a telephoto lens to get closer if needed.

- **Fill the field**— Use the field finder on the camera and completely fill the picture with the product. Again, get close to the subject!

- **Watch where you stand**— Don't shoot pictures into light. The light meter of a camera adjusts for the brightest light, often making the real subject of the picture too dark.

- **Watch your background**— Most people look a little strange with a flower arrangement for a hat or a pole growing out of their heads!

- **Use a tripod**— Tripods keep your work steady and prevent blurry pictures.

- **Consider getting a special camera holder**— If you will be taking lots of still shots of products sitting on a table, make a $35 investment in a camera holder specifically designed for taking overhead pictures.

Using Video

Video can be used when you want to show examples of yourself in action. Video takes pictures and adds sound. Keep in mind that no one really enjoys watching home videos, so keep your video short, to the point, and make it worth watching. Limit your video to 30 seconds to 3 minutes.Videos are usually given to an interviewer to review at a later time and are not used during the interview. Videos should be clearly labeled with your name, the content and purpose of the video, and the length.

Tips for Better Videos

Tips for photos also apply to video.

- **Emphasize your skills—** Keep the emphasis of your video on your skills, not on your production abilities.
- **Be prepared—** Always test out equipment ahead of time, especially if you are borrowing the equipment. It's always good to have extra batteries and an extension cord handy.
- **Watch your lighting—** Make sure the lighting is correct.
- **Label the video—** Indicate your name, the subject, and the length of video clips.

Tips for Looking Your Best in Front of a Lens

Your looks:

- **Get a good night's rest—** Weariness and stress are visible. Makeup can only cover so much. You want to avoid shiny foreheads and noses.
- **Make sure your hair looks neat and attractive—** If you need a haircut, get one several days in advance.
- **Gentlemen, be careful shaving, avoid scrapes and cuts—** Watch out for "five o'clock shadow."
- **Women— Wear makeup as usual.** If you wear heavy liner on your lower eyelid—go lightly or avoid it.

Clothing choices:

- Wear a proper fitting suit and shirt.
- Darker tones make the body look thinner.
- Avoid navy blue. It shows everything and appears murky.
- Avoid wearing black and white in color photos.
- Avoid turtleneck shirts and sweaters.
- Avoid wearing a white shirt. It can produce a glare.

- Wear a suit jacket for a serious look. Button the top button on all double-breasted suits.

- Make sure your clothes are not too tight. If you have recently gained weight, a new larger shirt will mask the gain better than a tight-fitting outfit.

- Neckties should look conservative unless the tie is part of a uniform look.

- Keep your jewelry to a minimum.

Production Tools—Copiers, Scanners, and Printers

Copiers, scanners, and printers are the most common tools you'll use to produce your portfolio. Here are some tips for making their output look as good as possible.

Copiers

- **Clean the machine—** Take a bottle of glass cleaner and a cloth with you the next time you go to make copies. Clean the glass on the machine and your final copies will be much clearer.

- **Align the paper—** Center the page on the copier and make sure the paper is straight on the copier. Nothing is more annoying than crooked copies!

- **Enlarge small fonts—** If the original document is in 10 point or smaller type, enlarge it to make it easier to read.

- **Copying small pieces of paper—** If you're copying something smaller than 8.5 by 11, be sure to put a white piece of paper behind the document so the background is clear. If necessary, tape the original to the paper to hold it centered. If you are trimming the copy from a larger size, be sure to use scissors. Think neat.

- **Color copying—** Color copying can be expensive. Look at the project and determine where you need color in your work samples. Use color copying when you want to accent something special. Certificates, awards, PowerPoint™ slides, and photos are good choices for color copying.

- **Consider scanning as an alternative**— While you can use a color copier to copy photographs, the quality may not be as good as you would like. Consider scanning color pictures for higher quality and then printing them on photo paper with a high quality color printer.
- **When in doubt, ask for professional help**— The staff at copy centers are usually happy to assist you with your copying.

Scanning Equipment

- **Scanners**— Scanners are a low-cost way of making color copies with your computer. Multifunction ink jet printers that can scan, copy, print, and fax are popular choices for home printers.
- **Resolution**— Scanning is measured in dpi—dots per inch. The higher the dpi, the more detailed and sharper the picture or document. Use no less than 300 dpi, preferably 600 dpi or higher, when scanning.

When scanning documents, set your resolution to 300 dpi minimum. They may take up more disk space, but the quality of your printout will be much better!

- **Scan certificates and degrees**— For a better look, consider scanning certificates and degrees; they copy official seals better than a copier.

Paper and Printing

Paper

As you choose the paper you'll use in your portfolio, keep in mind that the main purpose of the paper is to enhance the text and graphics in the document, making it easier to read. It can also be used to distinguish you from other people and can capture a bit of your style. Here are some guidelines for selecting paper:

- **Use high-quality, 24-lb. paper—** Heavier weight paper has a better feel and look. It also helps keep printing from showing through to the other side.

- **Paper color—** Use subtle colors, nothing harsh. Use the same paper consistently throughout the portfolio. Use color to draw attention to items you want to emphasize or to title pages. Don't overuse colored paper; limit yourself to a maximum of three different colors. White should be your primary color. Make sure your résumé is printed on white paper.

Follow the guidelines in this section and you're sure to have a fantastic looking portfolio! Putting the effort into making your portfolio look professional will pay off in your interviews and reflect the quality back onto you.

9. Model Job Descriptions in Dietetics

The following pages display common job titles and skills in the dietetic field.

Dietary Manager

Alternate Job Titles:	**corporate account manager; director of nutrition; school food service director**

Key Skills and Performance Areas

- Directs and coordinates food service activities
- Food service operations manager
- Ensures menus and department policies conform to nutritional standards, government/establishment regulations and procedures
- Quality control of patient diet management
- Plans and coordinates standards and procedures of:
  - Food storage
  - Preparation
  - Service
  - Equipment and department sanitation
  - Employee safety
  - Personnel policies and procedures
- Deploys food safety, sanitation, and quality standards
- Interacts with institutional administration to improve food service
- Computes operating costs
- Dietetic competency certificate.

Food Service Dietitian

Alternate Job Titles:	food service manager

Key Skills and Performance Areas

- Overall operation of establishment including:
  - ▲ Purchase food
  - ▲ Select and plan menus
  - ▲ Oversee staffing of kitchen and dining room operations
  - ▲ Maintain health, safety and sanitation levels.
- Establish standards for personnel performance, service to customers, menu rates, and advertising and publicity
- Purchase food and equipment
- Inspect the premises to maintain health, safety and sanitation regulations
- Estimate cost of food and beverage
- Requisition or purchase supplies
- Interact with customers and vendors
- Perform detailed clerical and financial duties such as:
  - ▲ Directing payroll operations
  - ▲ Handling large sums of money
  - ▲ Taking inventory
- Supervise a sales and advertising staff in large establishments
- Handle problems and cope with the unexpected and daily tasks.

Chief Clinical Dietitian

Alternate Job Titles: **clinical nutrition manager; dietitian; administrative director in dietetics department**

Key Skills and Performance Areas

- Administers, plans, and directs activities of a health-care center's nutrition department
- Establishes policies and procedures, and provides administrative direction for:
  - Menu formulation
  - Food preparation
  - Food service
  - Purchasing
  - Food safety and sanitation
  - Staffing and scheduling
- Hires dietetic staff, RDs, DTRs, and other necessary staff
- Directs departmental education programs
- Coordinates interdepartmental professional activities
- Consults management on matters pertaining to dietetics.

Clinical Dietitian

Alternate Job Titles: registered dietitian; long-term care dietitian; outpatient dietitian; pediatric dietitian, medical nutrition therapist

Key Skills and Performance Areas

- Plans therapeutic diets
- Implements preparation and service of meals for patients
- Consults with physician and other health-care personnel to determine nutritional needs and diet restrictions
- Formulates menus for therapeutic diets based on medical and physical conditions of patients
- Integrates patients' menus with basic institutional menus
- Inspects meals served for conformance to prescribed diets and for standards of palatability and appearance
- Instructs patients and their families in:
  - ▲ Nutritional principles
  - ▲ Dietary plans
  - ▲ Food selection
  - ▲ Food preparation
- May engage in research

Consultant Dietitian

Alternate Job Titles: institutional nutrition consultant

Key Skills and Performance Areas

- Advises and assists personnel in public and private establishments in food service systems and nutritional care of clients

- Makes recommendations for conformance level that will provide nutritionally adequate, quality food
- Plans, organizes, and conducts orientation and in-service educational programs for food service personnel
- Develops menu plans
- Assesses, develops, implements, and evaluates nutritional-care plans and provides for follow-up
- Ability to write proposals and reports
- Consults with health-care team concerning nutritional care of client

Research Dietitian

Alternate Job Titles: **research nutritionist; clinical research dietitian**

Key Skills and Performance Areas

- Conducts nutritional research to expand knowledge in one or more phases of dietetics
- Plans, organizes, and conducts programs in nutrition, foods, and food service systems, evaluating and utilizing appropriate methodology
- Studies and analyzes recent scientific discoveries in nutrition for:
  - ▲ Application in current research
  - ▲ Development of tools for future research
  - ▲ Interpretation to public
- Communicates findings through reports and publications.

Teaching Dietitian

Alternate Job Titles:	**dietetic internship director; cooperative extension educator; public health nutritionist; didactic program director; preceptor; professor (assistant, associate, or full)**

Key Skills and Performance Areas

- Plans, organizes, and conducts educational programs in dietetics, nutrition, and institution management for dietetic interns and nutrition majors; may include nursing students, and other medical personnel
- Develops curricula
- Prepares manuals, visual aids, course outlines, and other material used in teaching
- Instructs students on:
  - ▲ Principles of nutrition
  - ▲ Menu planning
  - ▲ Medical nutrition therapy
  - ▲ Food service operations
  - ▲ Food cost control
  - ▲ Marketing
  - ▲ Administration of dietary department
- May engage in research.

Dietetic Technician

Alternate Job Titles:	**None**

Key Skills and Performance Areas

- Provides services in assigned areas of food service management
- Teaches principles of food and nutrition

- Provides dietary consultation under direction of dietitian
- Plans menus based on established guidelines
- Standardizes recipes and tests new products for use in facility
- Supervises food production and service
- Obtains and evaluates dietary histories of individuals to plan nutritional programs
- Guides individuals and families in food selection, preparation, and menu planning, based upon nutritional needs
- Assists in referrals for continuity of patient care
- May select, schedule, and conduct orientation and in-service education programs
- May develop job specifications, job descriptions, and work schedules
- May assist in implementing established cost control procedures.

Chief Clinical Dietitian

Alternate Job Titles:	clinical nutrition manager; dietitian; administrative director in dietetics department

Key Skills and Performance Areas
- Administers, plans, and directs activities of a health-care center's nutrition department
- Establishes policies and procedures, and provides administrative direction for:
  - ▲ Menu formulation
  - ▲ Food preparation
  - ▲ Food service
  - ▲ Purchasing
  - ▲ Food safety and sanitation
  - ▲ Staffing and scheduling
- Hires dietetic staff, RDs, DTRs, and other necessary staff

- Directs departmental education programs
- Coordinates interdepartmental professional activities
- Consults management on matters pertaining to dietetics.

Sports Dietitian

Alternate Job Titles:	**Director of Performance Nutrition, Performance Dietitian, Nutrition Coach**

Key Skills and Performance Areas

- Provides individual and group/team nutrition counseling and education to enhance the performance of competitive and recreational athletes, on-site and during travel
- Counseling individuals and groups on daily nutrition for performance and health
- Translating the latest scientific evidence into practical sports nutrition recommendations
- Counsels athletes on optimal nutrition for exercise training (match nutrition to training phases and goals), competition, recovery from exercise, weight management, hydration, immunity, disordered eating, travel, and supplementation
- Serving as a food and nutrition resource for coaches, trainers, and parents
- Counsels athletes on optimal nutrition for recovery from illness or injury
  Providing sports nutrition education for health/wellness programs, athletic teams, and community groups
- Maintaining professional competency and skills required for professional practice
- Provides personalized meal and snack plans to promote achieving short- and long-term goals for athletic performance and good health.

10. Dietetics Work Samples

Here's a list of possible dietetic related work samples you might include in your career portfolio:

Tabbed Area of Portfolio	Possible Work Samples
Patient Education	■ Patient handouts ■ Preservation materials ■ Web research ■ Patient comprehension forms ■ Feedback sheets.
Food Service	■ Menu(s) you have designed ■ Food safety certification ■ Patient satisfaction ■ Photos of yourself working in the kitchen ■ Standard operating procedures developed ■ List of equipment you can operate with your supervisor's sign off.
Management	■ Schedules written ■ Performance evaluations ■ Forms you have created to assist staff ■ Committee reports and presentations.
Finance	■ Purchasing forms ■ Portion control systems developed ■ Inventory systems created ■ Budgets developed ■ Forecasts developed.
Clinical	■ Nutrient calculation sheets ■ Software applications you are trained on ■ Patient assessment forms ■ Patient consultation forms.
Research Methods	■ Methodology ■ Reports written ■ Photos of poster presentations ■ Publications ■ Proposals written.

11. Common Dietetics Professional Abbreviations

(Compiled by Kyle Shadix)

ADAF	ADA Foundation
BOD	Board of Directors
BSN	Bachelor of Science in Nursing
CADE	Commission on Accreditation for Dietetics Education
CCC	Certified Chef de Cuisine
CCE	Certified Culinary Educator
CEC	Certified Executive Chef
CD	Certified Dietitian
CCN	Certified Clinical Nutritionist
CDE	Certified Diabetes Educator
CDM	Certified Dietary Manager
CDHCF	Consultant Dietitians in Health Care Facilities DPG
CDN	Certified Dietitian Nutritionist
CDR	Commission on Dietetic Registration
CNM	Clinical Nutrition Manager
CNSD	Certified Nutrition Support Dietitian
COE	Council on Education
COP	Council on Practice
CP	Coordinated Programs
CPI	Council on Professional Issues
CSP	Certified Specialist in Pediatric Nutrition
CSR	Certified Specialist in Renal Nutrition
DBC	Dietitians in Business and Communications DPG
DCE	Diabetes Care and Education DPG
DDPD	Dietetics in Development and Psychiatric Disorders DPG
DEP	Dietetic Educators of Practitioners DPG
DHHS	Department of Health and Human Services
DMA	Dietary Managers Association

DNS	Dietitians in Nutrition Support DPG
DPG	Dietetic Practice Group
DT	Dietetic Technician
DTR	Dietetic Technician, Registered
EdD	Doctor of Education
FADA	Fellow of The American Dietetic Association
FCP	Food and Culinary Professionals DPG
FNCE	Food and Nutrition Conference and Exhibition
GN	Gerontological Nutritionists DPG
HEN	Hunger and Environmental Nutrition DPG
HOD	House of Delegates
JCAHO	Joint Commission on Accreditation of Healthcare Organizations
JADA	Journal of The American Dietetic Association
LD	Licensed Dietitian
LDN	Licensed Dietitian/Nutritionist
LN	Licensed Nutritionist
LNC	Legislative Network Coordinator
LPPC	Legislative and Public Policy Committee
LTC	Long-Term Care
MBA	Master of Business Administration
MEd	Master of Education
MMSc	Master of Medical Science
MNS	Master of Nutritional Science
MNT	Medical Nutrition Therapy
MPA	Master of Public Administration
MPH	Master of Public Health
MTS	Master of Theology Studies
NCND	National Center for Nutrition and Dietetics
NE	Nutrition Entrepreneurs DPG
NNM	National Nutrition Month

NST	Nutrition Support Therapist
ON	Oncology Nutrition DPG
PhD	Doctor of Philosophy
PN	Pediatric Nutrition DPG
QA	Quality Assurance
QM	Quality Management
RYDY	Recognized Young Dietitian of the Year
SCAN	Sports, Cardiovascular, and Wellness Nutritionists DPG
RD	Registered Dietitian
SPRC	State Professional Recruitment Coordinator

12. Core Competencies for the RD

From ACEND® Accreditation Standards for Dietitian Education Programs – ©2013 Accreditation Council for Education in Nutrition and Dietetics of the Academy of Nutrition and Dietetics

KRD #1: Scientific and Evidence Base of Practice

Competency	Key Content
Scientific and Evidence Base of Practice: Integration of scientific information and research into practice	Using Scientific and Evidenced-based practice to:
CRD 1.1 Select indicators of program quality and/or customer service and measure achievement of objectives.	Measure program quality
CRD 1.2 Apply evidence-based guidelines, systematic reviews and scientific literature (such as the Academy's Evidence Analysis Library and Evidence-based Nutrition Practice Guidelines, the Cochrane Database of Systematic Reviews and the U.S. Department of Health and Human Services, Agency for Healthcare Research and Quality, National Guideline Clearinghouse Web sites) in the nutrition care process and model and other areas of dietetics practice.	Use guidelines in the dietetic practice
CRD 1.3 Justify programs, products, services and care using appropriate evidence or data	Justify programs, products, and services
CRD 1.4 Evaluate emerging research for application in dietetics practice	Evaluate new research for its use in dietetics
CRD 1.5 Conduct research projects using appropriate research methods, ethical procedures and statistical analysis	Conduct research

KRD #2: Professional Practice Expectations

Competency		Key Content
Professional Practice Expectations: beliefs, values, attitudes and behaviors for the professional dietitian level of practice.		**Being a professional**
CRD 2.1	Practice in compliance with current federal regulations and state statutes and rules, as applicable and in accordance with accreditation standards and the Scope of Dietetics Practice and Code of Ethics for the Profession of Dietetics	Comply to rules and regulations
CRD 2.2	Demonstrate professional writing skills in preparing professional communications	Show writing skills
CRD 2.3	Design, implement and evaluate presentations to a target audience	Create and present presentations
CRD 2.4	Use effective education and counseling skills to facilitate behavior change	Counseling skills
CRD 2.5	Demonstrate active participation, teamwork and contributions in group settings	Be a team player
CRD 2.6	Assign appropriate patient care activities to DTRs and/or support personnel as appropriate	Delegate responsibilities
CRD 2.7	Refer clients and patients to other professionals and services when needs are beyond individual scope of practice	Refer clients to other resources when needed
CRD 2.8	Apply leadership principles achieve desired outcomes	Be a leader
CRD 2.9	Participate in professional and community organizations	Join professional and community organizations

CRD 2.10	Establish collaborative relationships with other health professionals and support personnel to deliver effective nutrition services	Network with other health professionals
CRD 2.11	Demonstrate professional attributes within various organizational cultures	Be professional
CRD 2.12	Perform self-assessment, develop goals and objectives and prepare a draft portfolio for professional development as defined by the Commission on Dietetics Registration	Create a CDR portfolio and keep up-to-date
CRD 2.13	Demonstrate negotiation skills	Negotiation skills

KRD #3: Clinical and Customer Services

Competency		Key Content
Clinical and Customer Services: Development and delivery of information, products and services to individuals, groups and populations		**Doing Your Job**
Perform the Nutrition Care Process (a through e below) and use standardized nutrition language for individuals, groups and populations of differing ages and health status, in a variety of settings		Follow the Nutritional Care Process below:
CRD 3.1.a	Assess the nutritional status of individuals, groups and populations in a variety of settings where nutrition care is or can be delivered	Assessment
CRD 3.1.b	Diagnose nutrition problems and create problem, etiology, signs and symptoms (PES) statements	Diagnose

CRD 3.1.c	Plan and implement nutrition interventions to include prioritizing the nutrition diagnosis, formulating a nutrition prescription, establishing goals and selecting and managing intervention	Plan and implement treatment
CRD 3.1.d	Monitor and evaluate problems, etiologies, signs, symptoms and the impact of interventions on the nutrition diagnosis	Monitor progress
CRD 3.1.e	Complete documentation that follows professional guidelines, guidelines required by health care systems and guidelines required by the practice setting.	Complete documentation
CRD 3.2	Demonstrate effective communications skills for clinical and customer services in a variety of formats	Use good communication skills
CRD 3.3	Develop and deliver products, programs or services that promote consumer health, wellness and lifestyle management	Deliver products, programs or services
CRD 3.4	Deliver respectful, science-based answers to consumer questions concerning emerging trends	Answer client questions about new trends
CRD 3.5	Coordinate procurement, production, distribution and service of goods and services	Coordinate services
CRD 3.6	Develop and evaluate recipes, formulas and menus for acceptability and affordability that accommodate the cultural diversity and health needs of various populations, groups and individuals	Evaluate recipes, formulas, and menus

KRD #4: Practice Management and Use of Resources

Competency		Key Content
Practice Management and Use of Resources: Strategic application of principles of management and systems in the provision of services to individuals and organizations		**Management**
CRD 4.1	Participate in management of human resources	HR
CRD 4.2	Perform management functions related to safety, security and sanitation that affect employees, customers, patients, facilities and food	Safety, security, sanitation
CRD 4.3	Participate in public policy activities, including both legislative and regulatory initiatives	Public policy
CRD 4.4	Conduct clinical and customer service quality management activities	Quality management
CRD 4.5	Use current informatics technology to develop, store, retrieve and disseminate information and data	Use technology
CRD 4.6	Analyze quality, financial or productivity data and develop a plan for intervention	Analyze data to create a plan
CRD 4.7	Propose and use procedures as appropriate to the practice setting to reduce waste and protect the environment	Sustainability
CRD 4.8	Conduct feasibility studies for products, programs or services with consideration of costs and benefits	Conduct feasibility studies
CRD 4.9	Analyze financial data to assess utilization of resources	Analyze finances

CRD 4.10	Develop a plan to provide or develop a product, program or service that includes a budget, staffing needs, equipment and supplies	Plan products, programs, and services
CRD 4.11	Code and bill for dietetic/nutrition services to obtain reimbursement from public or private insurers	Insurance billing

Glossary

ability– qualities that enable you to perform a task - something you have within you that helps you do the skill

academic plan of study– the course catalog description of an academic program with a breakdown of individual courses required for graduation

action verbs– verbs which are used on a résumé to describe what you have done

admissions interview- a meeting with representatives of a school to learn about their programs and explain what you have to offer

application letter– a letter sent to an employer indicating why you are qualified for the position and why you should be selected for an interview

awareness– a measure of skill where a person has recognition of a knowledge/skill, and has completed a task at least once

business card sheet– a blank sheet of card stock weight paper, perforated to create 10 separate cards – used for creating work sample overview cards

career– a series of related jobs where the skills you learn on one job can help you advance to jobs requiring more experience and advanced skills

career goals– performance achievements you set for yourself over a 2-5 year period

career objective– an overview of the kind of work you want to do: a one-or two-sentence summary of your career goals

career planning tool– a downloadable template used to help identify skills and work samples

career portfolio– an organized presentation of your knowledge, skills, and abilities; it can be in a hard copy or electronic format

career summary– career summary consists of two to three sentences which briefly outline your career history

CEU (Continuing Education Unit) – formal credit received for pursuing additional education as a professional.

CRD - Competency for Registered Dietitian– a set of skill competencies required for becoming a registered dietitian, set forth by ACEND$^®$, the credentialing board of the Academy of Nutrition and Dietetics

certifications– an acknowledgment by an institution or organization that you have a specific set of knowledge and skills

chronological résumé– résumé where the information is organized by date; information is listed in order of time elapsed, with the most recent experiences first; this is the most common and straight forward résumé format

collateral career portfolio– a hard copy printed portfolio

community service– volunteering your time and effort to a specific nonprofit organization

competencies– the ability to use your skills, abilities, work experience, interests, work values, and knowledge to do a job

competency model– a collection of competencies needed to work in a specific industry or do a particular job.

course tracking tool– a downloadable template used to help identify skills and work samples generated in a class

cover letter– cover letter is an e-mail or formal letter that is sent with the résumé and should briefly explain what sets you apart from others and why you would be the best person for the job

crosslinked work sample– a work sample that shows skills used in multiple areas

digital identify– how you appear online to other people, based on the information that can be found about you on the internet

downloadable templates– a series of templates that can be downloaded to assist in the development of several of the forms in this book; see the Resources section for more information

dpi (dots per inch) – a unit of measurement identifying the size and detail of an electronic image; the higher the dpi, the higher the quality, and the larger the file size

electronic résumé – a résumé designed for on screen viewing; often contains hyperlinks to work samples

ePortfolio– an organized presentation of your knowledge, skills, and abilities designed to be viewed online or on a computer

eRésumé – an electronic résumé designed for on screen viewing; often contains hyperlinks to work samples

evaluative interviews – an admissions interview where the results are used to help the school assess your qualifications as a candidate for their school

extra-wide 3-ring tabs with labels– page protectors that are wider than ordinary 3-ring tabs

faculty and employer biographies– brief descriptions of the people whose names appear throughout the portfolio-who they are and what they do

functional résumé– a résumé designed to highlight accomplishments and specific skills; organized by the different kinds of skills you can perform, such as management skills, marketing, finance, etc.

goals– performance achievements you set for yourself over a certain period

hard copy career portfolio– an organized presentation of your knowledge, skills, and abilities printed and presented in a 3-ring binder

hard skill– a practical skill, like working with computers or operating equipment and machinery

html– programming code used to display a web page

hyperlink– a highlighted or underlined word in a document that when clicked takes you to a web page

inquiry letter– a cover letter written to a company who has not advertised any job openings

informational interview – a school admissions interview designed to give you more information about the school, where the interview is not used to make admissions decisions.

internship career portfolio– a career portfolio used to compete for internships with special emphasis on your coursework and academic record

job– a position or work that brings in money or helps you build your career

key skill area– tabbed sections containing information on the different types of skills you want to promote such as management, training, professional skills related to your field, communications, etc.

keywords– keywords are terms that cue people into specific skills and abilities

knowledge– something that you have learned or discovered

KRD - Knowledge for Registered Dietitian– a set of knowledge areas required for becoming a registered dietitian, set forth by ACEND®, the credentialing board of the Academy of Nutrition and Dietetics

KSAs– acronym for knowledge, skills, and abilities

learning agreement– a list of goals and objectives you plan to achieve while employed as an intern

letter of introduction– a letter highlighting your positive points which is written to a specific person who is generally known by the writer

letter of recommendation– letter of support or reference from people who can verify your abilities in a skill area

letter of support– a letter that provides proof of your abilities and character from someone who knows you well

management philosophy– a brief description of your beliefs about yourself and your profession

mastery– a measure of skill indicating the ability to consistently perform the task without effort

networking letter– a letter used to request job search advice and assistance from your connections

online profile– a statement written to appear online giving people a brief overview of who you are and what you have to offer

pdf – an electronic document format for transferring and viewing documents; Adobe Acrobat Viewer is required for viewing the image online

performance career portfolio– a career portfolio designed to be used on the job, once you have been hired

performance résumé– a résumé that lists employment information in a chronological format, then organizes the skills you've developed in each position in order to highlight your accomplishments

photo sheet holder– 3-hole punched plastic sheet protectors designed to hold 3x5 or 6x4 photos

practicing– a measure of skill indicating the ability to follow a guide to complete a task

prerequisites– courses that you have to take first before you can take a more advanced class

professional career portfolio– a career created for the purpose of getting a job

professional membership– participation in a nonprofit organization related to a specific career area or field of study

prospecting letter– a letter sent to companies to let them know you are interested in jobs that may be currently open or become available in the future

rare talent– a valuable skill that sets you apart from others

references– a list of people who can verify your character, academic record, or employment history

referral cover letter– a letter written by someone who knows you, to their friend or colleague, introducing you and highlighting your positive points

résumé– a document that gives general information on your work history, education, activities, memberships and community service, and highlights your skills and achievements

sheet protectors– clear, plastic, 3-hole punched pockets that hold documents and work samples

skill– the ability to perform a task - usually something learned

skill areas– tabbed sections containing information on the different types of skills you want to promote such as management, training, professional skills related to your field, communications, etc.

skill gap– the difference between your current skills and the skills needed for a particular job situation

skill harvesting– employers post multiple jobs positions and hire one person whose skills match best to more than one position

skill résumé– a résumé designed to highlight accomplishments and specific skills; it is organized by the different kinds of skills you can perform, such as management skills, marketing, finance, etc.

skill sets– checklists of critical skills related to a specific area of expertise; your level of skill is documented with a signature from an employer or instructor who can validate your work

soft skills– a broader range of skills related to your personality and attitudes

statement of originality – a paragraph placed at the front of your career portfolio stating this is your work and asking viewers to keep it confidential

summary sheet– a page placed at the beginning of a tabbed section of the career portfolio listing the samples included in the section

tab page– a tabbed divider used to indicate the start of a new section in the career portfolio

tabs– plastic sheets or stick-on indexes that fit on the side of a sheet protector to divide different sections of your career portfolio

technical skill– relate to practical skills, like working with computers or operating equipment and machinery

technology– software and information technology used to perform a task or do a job

tools– machines, equipment, and tools you may use on the job

top grading– an employment practice where each employee is assigned a grade based on their perceived value to the company

transferable skills– skills you've gathered through various jobs, volunteer work, hobbies, sports, or other life experiences that can be used in a different setting

volunteer experience– donating your time and effort to a specific nonprofit organization

web presence– how you appear online to other people, based on the information that can be found about you on the internet

work philosophy – a brief description of your beliefs about yourself and your profession

work sample overview cards– a small business card created for each sample to help a viewer quickly identify the type of sample and what it represents; the card is slid into the sheet protector and floats over the top of the sample

work samples– physical examples of your work including: projects, reports, documents, pictures, letters, case studies, education materials, work flow analyses, or projects completed while on the job

works in progress– a brief list of work, activities, projects, or efforts you are in the process of completing

Index

spell checking 164
    text 161–165
summary sheets 101–103
supply list 109, 148
    for emergency development 149

T

tabs 99, 110, 150, 170
    community service 10
    key skill areas 66
    organizing 109–112
    reference information 9
    works in progress 10
teaching dietitian 176
technical skills 18, 19–20
technology 20
templates 100, 119
    academic planner tool 34–35
    career planning tool 26–27, 32, 64, 159, 189
    coursework tracking tool 27, 62
    faculty employer bios 104
    recommendation request 58
    references 106
    skill sets 62
    statement of originality 101, 103
    work philosophy and goals 34, 38
    work sample overview cards 67
text 161–164
    elements of 162
    tips for using 161–162
tools 20
transferable skills 19, 22–24
    list of 155–158

U

U.S. Department of Labor
    SCANS 154

V

video 166–168
    tips for appearance 167
    tips for clothing 167–168
volunteerism. See community service

W

web presence 89–90
work philosophy 9, 36–38, 101, 103, 150
work philosophy and goals
    template 34, 38
work samples 39–68
    academic 46
    choosing 107–108
    community service 49
    confidentiality of 52
    creating 52–62
    dietetic examples 179
    job 46
    letters of recommendation 57–58
    list of 179
    overview cards 66–67
        template 67
    rules for using 44–108
    saving 63–66
    sources of 44–52
    types of 40, 44
works in progress 10